ISAAC ROOP

Pioneer & Political Leader of Northeastern California

by James Thomas Butler

Introduction by Zellamae Miles

A LASSEN COUNTY HISTORICAL SOCIETY BOOK
published by
HIGH DESERT PRESS, JANESVILLE, CA

Isaac Roop: Pioneer & Political Leader of Northeastern California

© 1994 by James Thomas Butler
All rights reserved

Cover artwork © 1994 by Ben Barker

Printed in the United States of America by Western Book/Journal Press

Library of Congress Number: 94-78246

ISBN: 0-936029-40-4

First edition: August 1994

10 9 8 7 6 5 4 3 2 1

ABOUT THE COVER: *The artwork on the cover of this book is a painting created by Susanville artist Ben Barker, which is now hanging in the Nevada State Capitol along with portraits of all of Nevada's previous governors. A special benefit dinner and unveiling ceremony, sponsored by the Lassen County Historical Society, was held on March 12, 1994; the following week the portrait was delivered to Carson City, Nevada. On March 29, 1994, Nevada officially accepted the portrait by passing a bill in the Assembly. In doing so, the State of Nevada has officially acknowledged Isaac Roop as their first Provisional Territorial Governor, 1859-61. In addition to the portrait, the Lassen County Historical Society also delivered the handmade custom frame, which was designed and constructed by Austin Meinert of Janesville, California.*

Isaac Newton Roop, 1822-69

Courtesy of Eastman's

TABLE OF CONTENTS

INTRODUCTION

Isaac Newton Roop was my great-grandfather, and his daughter, Susan (for whom Susanville is named), was my grandmother. I never knew Susan Roop-Arnold, but as a young girl, I would enjoy the stories my father, Medford "Med" Arnold, would tell about both her and Isaac, particularly those stories that illustrated what community-minded people my ancestors were.

On behalf of the Roop-Arnold family, I want to thank Mr. James Thomas Butler for writing this book. Collecting the information contained in these pages was something my family wanted to do for many, many years, but for whatever reasons, it never got done. For his thorough research of Isaac Roop's life, my family will always be indebted to Mr. Butler.

Also, I would like to extend a special thank you to Mrs. Janet Corey, President of the Lassen County Historical Society, for deciding to have this book published. Janet, for all she has done for the Roop-Arnold family, especially her hard work and determination in getting the State of Nevada to give Isaac Roop the recognition he was due, will always hold a special place in all our hearts.

Zellamae Miles

Susanville, CA, August 1994

ACKNOWLEDGMENTS

The publication of this book has been a long time in coming. Along the way, many fine and talented people have been involved. We would like to take this opportunity to thank some of those people for their help and support.

This book is Brian Bauman's second editorial assignment, and his skills have been greatly appreciated by us all. The same can be said for our proofreader, Liz Fitton; she puts a lot of time and care into her work, and it shows whenever we receive back her noted pages. And, of course, we wouldn't even have this book if Gwen Pacheco hadn't provided her computer/typing skills early on.

A very special thank you goes to artist Ben Barker for allowing us to use his new portrait of Isaac Roop on the cover of this book. The portrait, which now hangs in the Nevada State Capitol, is a beautiful work of art, and we are proud to have it appear on the cover.

Finally, we want to thank Faye Messinger for letting us have access to her copy of the Roop House Register, Lois Mankins for providing all of the black & white photo processing, and Debbie Cleveland of *Picture Perfect...Custom Framing* in Susanville for assisting with the preparation of the illustrations.

High Desert Press
Janesville, CA, August 1994

LISTING OF ILLUSTRATIONS

Map

CHAPTER ONE
HEADING FOR SHASTA

Isaac Roop was the first settler in the area of northern California which lies east of the Sierra Nevada Mountains. The log house which he built in Honey Lake Valley was the first permanent habitation in the area. Chiefly through his efforts, a settlement grew around it and today the town he founded, Susanville, is the largest in that out-of-the-way section of the state.

Isaac Roop played a prominent role in every early movement to provide adequate government for the area, which was in an anomalous position, both geographically and politically. His name is inextricably bound to the early history of northeastern California and the entire eastern slope of the Sierra. Although American historians have extensively examined the era of American settlement of California, no one has done a specific study of Isaac Roop.

The migrants to California came in great numbers and, unlike most frontier or migrant groups, penned an abundance of source material, which is still extant. Drawing upon this abundance, historians have uncovered much detail and filled in gaps in the total picture. They have had the opportunity to extend their work into localized studies, recording and interpreting events and the movement of personages with care and perfection. And yet, they have not told the whole story. Lack of readily available materials applies especially to the pioneer years of some of the outlying areas of the state. Although one may consider research in such areas as bordering on mere local history, it is actually more than that. The early leaders of these pioneer settlements deserve investigation. They cannot be relegated to obscurity merely because of inaccessibility of materials about them. Someone must make studies of each of them, and, whether raising or lowering their historical importance, attempt to give a just evaluation based upon research. Isaac Roop deserves such a study.

Born on March 13, 1822, in Carroll County, Maryland,[1] Isaac Roop was the fifth of nine sons and two daughters born to Joseph and Susan Engle Roop.[2] On his father's side, he was a descendant of five generations of German-Americans.[3] The Roop name has actually come from the anglicization of the German pronunciation of Rupp. This name has been traced back to the Rhine Valley and also to the Anabaptists in Rome, Switzerland, in the 1520s.[4] The American ancestors of Isaac Roop were a part of the German element of the colonial frontier population. They lived in New York at the end of the seventeenth century and within two generations had moved southwest to Lancaster, Pennsylvania.[5] Shortly after the American Revolution, Isaac's grandfather, the elder Joseph Roop, moved across the Susquehanna River to Carroll County, Maryland.[6] There he and his family settled. Young Joseph grew up, married and began to raise his large family. To support it he farmed and raised stock.[7] Isaac, like the other children, grew up on the farm and began working at a very early age. He received little formal education.[8]

Isaac Roop's father was not unlike his ancestors or the frontier farmers who lived about him. Tiring of Maryland, he decided to pull up his roots and head for new opportunity in the West. In 1838, when Isaac was sixteen, Joseph Roop relocated to Ashland County, Ohio.[9]

Joseph Roop was an industrious man and soon grew relatively prosperous.[10] However, his main interest was not financial but religious wealth. He was a practicing Dunkard, wearing plain clothes and a beard.[11] As soon as he was able, he gave a grant of land to his church, and "the Dickey Church of the Brethren, 2 miles south of Ashland, still occupies land that he contributed."[12]

Shortly after moving to Ohio, Isaac felt it was time to go out on his own. Probably with the aid of his father, he went into his first business, a saw and grist mill.[13] Once he was established, Isaac began looking about for a wife. His search was fruitful, for he met Miss Nancy Gardner, who was just nine months younger than himself. On December 24, 1840, two days after Nancy Gardner's eighteenth birthday, they were married.[14]

Isaac's bride had a family background similar to that of Isaac. Her father, John Gardner, had migrated from Germany to Allegheny, Pennsylvania, where his daughter was born. He moved to Ashland soon after.[15] For a time he sent Nancy to Transylvania College.[16]

The newlyweds settled on a farm adjoining Joseph Roop's land. Isaac continued to operate his mill. Realizing the importance of gaining the education he had missed, he spent his spare hours studying under the tutelage of his wife. He learned to read and write and eventually mastered the essentials of a basic education.[17]

Isaac Roop and his wife had three children, each born in November of the odd years beginning in 1841. They were Susan, John and Isaiah.[18] His peaceful rural life abruptly ended in the spring of 1850. Nancy Gardner Roop contracted typhoid fever and died on June 20.[19] In his grief, Isaac could not bear to remain in Ohio. By September 9, 1850, he had concluded his business affairs, left his children with their grandparents and started for California.[20]

Isaac Roop was not the first of the family to arrive in California. Josiah, an elder brother, came sometime in 1849. J. G. Bruff refers to a Mr. Roop, whom he first met on the Belle Creole heading up the Missouri River in May, 1849, on the way to California. Bruff recorded this information at their second meeting in

November, 1850, when he also noted that Roop was now a successful trader at "Redding's Diggings," at the head of the Sacramento Valley.[21] Undoubtedly this was Josiah Roop, for another source shows that, prior to 1851, he had established a general merchandise store at Shasta (known as Readings' or Readings' Diggings in 1849).[22]

Isaac Roop came to California by sea. He crossed the isthmus at Nicaragua and arrived in San Francisco on the steamship Oregon on October 18, 1850.[23] This arrival of the Oregon is better remembered as the one which brought news of the admission of California to the Union.[24] From San Francisco, Roop traveled north to the Shasta region.[25]

As was the case in much of California, the miners had only recently swarmed into the Shasta area. It had been little but virgin land only a few years before. Trappers and hunters had traversed the northern portion of California throughout the Mexican period, but the first settlement had not been made until five years before Roop arrived. The man who lays claim to being the first settler of the Shasta region is Pierson B. Reading.[26]

As a member of the well known Chiles-Walker party, Reading started from Missouri for California in 1843. At Fort Hall, the group divided, with Joseph Walker heading south to cross the Sierra Nevadas through the pass which bears his name, and Joseph Chiles and the group including Reading going to Oregon, then down into California by way of Goose Lake and the Pit River. They reached the Sacramento River at Cottonwood Creek, and went on to Sutter's Fort, arriving on November 10, 1843.[27]

Reading, like some other Americans who came overland early in the 1840s, became associated with John Sutter at his fort. Through Sutter's influence, Reading was able to obtain a grant for a ranch far up the Sacramento, near where he first saw the stream. Governor Micheltorena made the grant to Reading in December, 1844. It included over 26,000 acres of land centering around Cottonwood Creek. Reading called his ranch Bueno Ventura, and settled it in 1845.

This was the northern-most of the grants during the Mexican period and the northern outpost of settlement before 1849.[28]

The plans of Reading, like those of thousands of others in California, were radically changed in the three years after Reading received his grant. The American aspirations toward California made themselves felt in 1846 by the activities of Fremont and Sloat and the Bear Flag Revolt, which anticipated the Mexican War. After the formal declaration of war reached California in July, the fighting became statewide. Although the American victory in California came early in 1847, the area did not become a part of the United States until the Treaty of Guadeloupe-Hidalgo on February 2, 1848.

The second great change of the late 1840s was the discovery of gold by James Marshall in January, 1848. Before the news had spread very far and the excitement enveloped the whole territory, Reading visited the site of the discovery at Coloma with Sutter.[29] Upon seeing the land, Reading felt that his ranch had similar soil which might yield gold.

Returning north, Reading began prospecting and made strikes along Cottonwood Creek and farther north on Clear Creek. Then he crossed the Coast Range to the Trinity River area where he made other discoveries. He returned there in 1849 and made his richest finds on the Trinity at a place which became known as Reading's Bar. Returning to the Sacramento Valley, he developed the workings along Clear Creek, one of which was at Reading's Springs, a spot which had previously been known as a camping place for travelers from Oregon.[30] The rush into the area began in the summer of 1849 and continued into the fall. By winter, there was a camp of 500 to 600 miners living in tents around Reading's Springs. The first house, one of logs, was put up in October, 1849, but the first frame buildings were not erected until that winter.[31] By spring, the town was taking on a look of permanency, with hotels, stores and saloons to provide for the necessities of the miners.

Gold was not the only factor in the development at Reading's Springs. Geography was to have nearly as important a role in the rise of the town. Lying near the end of the Sacramento Valley, it became the point of entrance to the whole group of northern towns, gulches, bars and flats which lay among the hills and valleys formed by the intermingling of the Coast Range with the westward jutting spurs of the Sierra. The mining areas from the nearby Trinity River north to the Scott, Klamath and Shasta Rivers were all within the commercial orbit of this town. A census in 1850 showed 278 "permanent" residents of the community,[32] while the immediate area abounded with camps along Clear Creek and off toward the Trinity diggings. In June, 1850, a citizens' meeting held on the main street voted to change the name of the town from Reading's Springs to Shasta.[33]

Josiah Roop was one of the men who took part in these activities of 1849 and 1850. He was well-established as a merchant in Shasta when Isaac arrived in October of 1850.

What may be the first reference to Isaac Roop after he landed in California appeared in the Sacramento Transcript of January 4, 1851. The writer of the article had met Josiah Roop, who was in Sacramento on business. Josiah, whom he describes as "a gentleman whose statements can be received with credence," informed him that mining along Scott's River was being done not by goldwashers or rockers, but by "panwashing and picking up lumps." Josiah further stated that "his brother made $4000 at the mines on Scott's River in the short time of two weeks...". The writer here includes a somewhat superfluous warning that "Mr. R. desires us to say, lest some might be misled, that his brother had a lucky claim, and that many who were there engaged were only realizing the average yields of miners in other sections of the country." He then concludes by giving the exact location. "The bar to which we have referred is about 4 miles from where Scott's River empties into the Klamath and 200 miles from the mouth of the latter river." This possible good fortune may have amounted to a sizeable stake for Isaac. Combined with any money he might have had from his days in Ohio, it was enough for him to establish himself in more conservative ventures.

"In 1850...the Oak Bottom Hotel, located seven miles from Shasta between Whiskeytown and the Tower House" was mortgaged by John Howell "... to Isaac

Roop for $2,800 with interest at three cents per month."[34] Roop remained there but a short time, for in June, 1851, he went to Shasta and "kept public house."[35] He still had business in Oak Bottom, however, and on one of his trips returning from Oak Bottom to Shasta, he had an encounter with a group of desperadoes. Seven men and two women--"persons of doubtful reputation"--had been expelled from Shasta the day before by its Vigilance Committee. The expulsion had been carried out shortly after the burning of a hay yard, worth a reported $30,000. The group was gathered outside of town, and as Roop passed by, one of them decided to take out his revenge upon him. The desperado fired a shot which luckily missed. When Roop got to Shasta, he reported the incident to the committee which then resolved to take the group in custody to the southern boundary of the county "...where they should be released and sent down river."[36]

In October of 1851, Roop "went to Bear River."[37] Undoubtedly this refers to Bear Creek, which is a tributary of the Sacramento some miles below Shasta.

In the first edition of the Shasta Courier, which came into print on March 12, 1852, Roop and two others inserted cards announcing their candidacy for the post of sheriff of Shasta County in a special election, the sheriff-elect having died.[38] No further item mentions Isaac Roop in connection with the election or the office. He may have withdrawn frorm the election in order to accept a job in the Shasta post office. One source says that Isaac Roop became the first postmaster of Shasta in March, 1852.[39] This is contrary to federal records which show that Robert W. Crenshaw was appointed the first postmaster of Shasta on July 10, 1851.[40] The Shasta Courier states that, early in 1852, Josiah Roop was the Shasta postmaster and Isaac Roop was his assistant.[41] So, after a year and a half of moving about, Isaac Roop had settled in Shasta and set about establishing himself as a prominent and stable citizen of the community.

Shasta itself was in the process of becoming stabilized. In the first years of American control of California, the old Mexican system of local government was retained, pending action from Washington upon statehood. Operating under this temporary arrangement, Shasta came under the jurisdiction of an *alcalde* from its inception until the organization of the state of California in September, 1850. Shasta was included in Shasta County, one of the original counties.[42] There were five townships in the original county: Shasta, Lower Springs, Clear Creek, Cottonwood and Weaver. In 1851, four new townships came into being: French Gulch, Fortunate (Oak Bottom), Scott (in Scott Valley), and Shasta Plains (part of the present area included in Siskiyou and Modoc counties). All of the first group centered around the areas tributary to the Sacramento or southern Trinity area, and the remainder of the county, which included most of northeastern California, went unorganized until the second set of townships was set up.

On February 10, 1851, the county court system was organized at Reading's Ranch, and it met the next day in Shasta to begin its term.[43] By January of the next year, Josiah Roop was one of the associate justices of this court.[44]

Shasta had grown rapidly from a tent camp of 1849 and the temporary town of 1850 to an active community with a weekly newspaper, numerous business houses and seven hotels. From the 278 figure of 1850, the population had risen to 3,448 by October of 1852.[45]

During this year, Josiah and Isaac Roop may have made an informal agreement admitting Isaac as a partner in Josiah's business. Originally Josiah had a partnership with B. H. Johnson.[46] They had operated a store and hotel in the "Old Dominion," a building on the main street of Shasta. On April 13, 1851, the partners severed their connection, and Josiah Roop became sole owner. On the books, he remained so permanently.[47]

Whether or not Josiah took his brother in as a formal partner, he knew he could rely on Isaac to administer his business for him if need be. In May 1852, Josiah took advantage of Isaac's presence to join a group of prominent men in Shasta who were going to travel to the "Atlantic States." Josiah planned to go to Ohio in order to bring his family to California.[48] He left his affairs in the hands of Isaac Roop and James N. Rhodes, and left Shasta for Ohio.[49]

The group was going by sea. They left San Francisco on May 18th and spent nine days crossing the isthmus. They then boarded the steamer Prometheus bound for New York. However, during the journey, Josiah had severe dysentery and, despite the aid of doctors, he died on board ship.[50] Isaac was informed of his brother's death in a letter of June 20, 1852, from State Senator Royal T. Sprague, one of the Shasta group on the ship.[51]

With the death of Josiah, Isaac, who had been acting postmaster, officially took the position after citizens of the town had circulated a petition in his behalf.[52]

Mail service improved rapidly during this period. In the spring of 1851, Baxter and Monroe established the first stage line into Shasta County.[53] While Josiah Roop was serving as postmaster, the first mail by stage was delivered May 8, 1852.[54] Also in May, the service of another stage line was added when Hall and Crandall advertised a daily mail stage, which took seventeen hours to cover the distance from Sacramento to Shasta.[55] This daily mail halted in the winter and was not resumed until the next April. In the April 23 issue of the Shasta Courier, Postmaster Isaac Roop and the Baxter and Company line of stages received the thanks of the editor for the additional service provided.

During the year ending March, 1853, Postmaster Roop received 41,263 letters. He delivered an average of 101 letters a day, but one out of every twelve he received had to be returned as dead letters.[56] This illustrates the rapid turnover of the population of the mining area.

The route to Sacramento was all-important for supplies and as a link with central California and areas outside the state. Equally important were the connections with the mines in the immediate Shasta area and to the north and west. This area provided Shasta's markets. But these close and convenient connections with the settled portions of the state were not the only ones the people of Shasta desired. In addition, the tradesmen saw a place for further extension of their markets by directing the great flow of immigration to California into a northern route, preferably with its terminus at Shasta. Most of the travel at this time was coming over more southerly routes, chiefly the Truckee and Walker Pass routes. The Lassen Trail, the most northerly route into California, had been used in 1849, but fell into disrepute because of its difficulty and length, and was little used after that year.

In the spring of 1851, a prospecting party including a William H. Nobles traveled directly east from Shasta, and, passing north of Mt. Lassen and through Honey Lake Valley,[57] entered the Great Basin.[58] Nobles was impressed with the route through the mountains and saw the commercial possibilities of a direct, easy route for immigration. He went to Shasta and, for the sum of $2,000, promised to show a northern route across the mountains which would be superior to all others. Businessmen raised the money, and a party of citizens accompanied Nobles on a trip to explore this route. They left Shasta May 3, 1852, and traveled east as far as the Humboldt River. Noting the rate of ascent and descent, distance between watering holes, amount of grass and similar necessary items, they reached the Humboldt in eight days.[59] Nobles--and his money--left the party there and continued east.[60]The results of the venture were encouraging to the Shasta citizens, for, compared to other options, this route was easy. There were no extremely high passes to cross, there was adequate water and grass, and above all, it was almost in a direct line from the bend of the Humboldt to Shasta.[61] The news of the better route soon spread and the flow of travel over it increased rapidly.

Roop was certainly interested in the new route. At the time, however, it did not dominate his thinking as it would later. His interests in 1852 were still in Shasta. As postmaster and one of the leading citizens of the town, Roop took a leading part in community affairs. He had become a Mason in June, 1851, in Sacramento and was a charter member of Western Star Lodge No. 2 of Shasta.[62] He was in charge of raising funds from Shasta for the Washington Monument.[63]

Politically, Roop was a Whig, and very active. In November, 1852, the Shasta County Whigs chose him to be president for the ensuing year.[64]He was their candidate for Shasta County Assessor, but he was defeated 836-674.[65] After his entrance into Whig political circles, the Shasta Courier, a Democratic paper, contained fewer and fewer complimentary mentions of Roop, as had been its custom in previous issues.

By order of the Probate Court of Shasta County, Roop became administrator of the estate of his deceased brother. Soon afterward, he gave notice of the auction of the property consisting of the "Old Dominion" and its lot, valued at $2,000, and across the street, another lot and building valued at $4,000. As a result of the Roops' use of it, the latter building had become known as the Post Office.[66] The Post Office property was disposed of, but the auction of the "Old Dominion" was postponed until April 9 and again until June 25.[67]

Shasta, during this period, was in the middle of its boom era, but Roop had decided not to be a part of it. The auctioning of his brother's property was followed by a notice in the June 11, 1853, issue of the Shasta Courier, stating his plans to leave Shasta. It read in part:

> HO! FOR SALT RIVER! I, Isaac Roop, Post Master in and for the city of Shasta, having been in office eighteen...long months, having fattened at the public crib and being a liberal man, am willing, and indeed anxious, to share the spoils of a good fat office, therefore I shall resign my office on the 30th inst., and recommend to the Democrats of this County the name of D.D. Harrill as Post Master, he being well qualified to fill the post and one in whom the Whigs as well as the Democrats have every confidence...
>
> I will be gone four years, it being my intention to leave for Salt River on the first day of July next, on the splendid and well known steamer "Bigler No. 2" For passage and freight apply on board, or to the undersigned.
>
> Isaac Roop,
Defunct P.M., Shasta

It is difficult to interpret the meaning of this notice. The Salt River mentioned may have referred to Salt Creek, a newly opened diggings northeast of Shasta. There are decided political overtones in the announcement of leaving on the steamer "Bigler No. 2." This is a play on the name of John Bigler, the incumbent Democratic Governor of California. At the time of this notice, Bigler was just completing his first term and was up for reelection. Since Bigler's defeat of their candidate, P. B. Reading, in the election of 1851,[68] the Whigs had been rapidly declining in influence throughout the state. Isaac may have seen any chances for his own political future fading with them.

The planned resignation, however, was never to take place. Three days after this notice appeared, fire broke in an unoccupied building on the main street of Shasta, spread in both directions, jumped the narrow street, and before it had burned itself out it had consumed seventy buildings including every hotel, store and saloon in town. About forty buildings remained in all of Shasta, mostly small residences and a few business houses at either end of town. Roop must have lost everything, and the estate of Josiah Roop was listed as losing $4,000.[69] The estimate of the total losses was $100,000 for buildings and $400,000 for personal property.[70] One source says that Roop let his buildings burn while he was fighting the fire where it started and saving the lives of the school children.[71] He managed to save the letters and books from the post office, although the building and all of its furniture burned. The next morning he opened the post office in a vacant building adjoining the boarding house.[72] In the citizens' meetings which were called to survey the damage, ascertain the cause of the fire and plan for the rebuilding of the town, Roop took a leading part, serving on committees and presiding at one of the meetings.[73]

The town was quickly rebuilt. The main street was widened and many brick buildings began to rise from the ashes. Roop had temporarily abandoned his plans to resign office and move from Shasta. The loss of his own property and that of his brother's estate had been a serious blow to him; however, another of a different nature was about to fall. The August 6, 1854 issue of the Shasta Courier contained the following editorial comment:

> On Wednesday last our fellow citizen, D.D. Harrill, Esq., received his appointment as Postmaster at this place vice Isaac Roop, removed. We understand that the appointment of Mr. Harrill bears date 20th April, and must have arrived at this office, by ordinary course of mail about the 5th of June at the farthest. If so, it has been laying in this office about two months, notwithstanding Mr. H. has frequently called for letters during that time. Indeed we have been assured that the fact of its being in the office at all, was ascertained

>altogether by accident.   There is something most
>discreditable to certain parties connected with this affair,
>if these things are so -- something very criminal.

What Roop's intentions were we shall never know, but it is doubtful, if he received the letter before June, that he should recommend Harrill for the job, and then keep the letter in the post office, save it from fire, and transfer it to the new post office, if he never intended to deliver it.   In view of the upcoming statewide elections, the article may have been a political attack aimed at Isaac Roop as a leader of the Whig party in the county.   Whatever the case, Roop could not complete his plan of looking elsewhere to make his living.

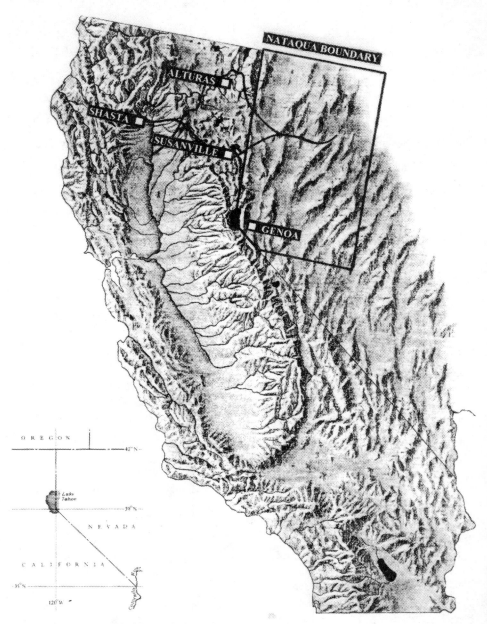

The Lassen Trail begins in the Nataqua Territory, travels northwest past Alturas, then turns southward and terminates along the Sacramento River south of Shasta. **Nobles' Road** also begins in Nataqua, but travels a more direct route past Susanville, then on to Shasta.

CHAPTER TWO
FOUNDING A SETTLEMENT

During August 1853, Isaac Roop packed some provisions, saddled a horse and rode east from Shasta into the mountains.[74] He followed Nobles' Road through the Sierras to the eastern slope, where he came upon fertile Honey Lake Valley. In September of 1853, he posted a claim at the head of the valley, along the bank of the Susan River.[75] Thus he became "the first white claimant to any part of California East of the Sierra."[76]

One can only theorize about the thoughts which passed through the mind of the 31 year old widower as he journeyed to Honey Lake and a new way of life. Roop's most practical move would have been to relocate in another of the growing settlements in California. There opportunity abounded. But Isaac Roop had behind him a background of five generations of rural German-American life. It is probable that this factor, in combination with his crushing misfortunes, convinced him that he had seen enough of life in the mining towns of California. The unsettled land to the east was more to his liking.

Notice

I, Isaac Roop do take up and Claim the following discribed tract of land. Begining at a pine tree on the South Side of Susan River at the foot of the Bluffs thence runing North some four hundred Roods more or less to a pine stake sett at the foot of the bluffs on the North side of Susan River thence West to the timber thence South a long said timber to the top of the Bluffs on the north of Susan River thence up said River on the top of said Bluffs two miles thence cross Susan River to the top of the Bluffs on the south side of Susan River thence down on the Edge of said Bluffs to the Edge of the timber thence to continue in a South Easterly bou(?) to the place of beginning. (this being In the head of the Valley)

    Sept. A.D. 1853.   Isaac Roop
    July A.D. 1854 Built a house on the above Claim
    Left for Shasta Nov. A.D. 1855.

                A. Tru Copy of the Origonal
This first day of May A.D. 1856 Isaac Roop Recdr

Notice

I the undersign Claim the Privelige to take all of the Water out of Smith Creek at the Junction of the two forks where this stake stands I shall build the dam some Six feet high and cary the Water along the south hill to the Emegrant Road   August A.D. 1854 Isaac Roop

Recorded this first day of May A.D. 1856

Isaac Roop Recd

Page One of Roop's Record Book

(See Page 17)

Notice

I Isaac Roop do take up and Claim the following
discribed tract of land. Begining at a pine tree
on the South Side of Susan River at the foot of
the Bluffs thence runing North Some four hundred
Roods most or less to a pine Stake sett at the foot
of the bluffs on the North Side of Susan River thence
West to the timber thence South a long said timber to the
top of the Bluffs on the North of Susan River thence up
Said River on the top of said Bluffs two miles thence cross
Susan River to the top of the Bluffs on the South Side of Susan
River thence thence down on the Edge of said Bluffs to the
Edge of the timber thence to continue in a South Ceasterley course
to the place of begining. (this being In the head of the Valley)
Sept AD 1853.   Isaac Roop
July AD 1854 Built a house on the above Claim
Left for Shasta Nov A.D. 1855.

A True Copy of the Original
This first day of May A.D. 1856   Isaac Roop Recor

Notice

I the undersign Claim the Privilige to take all of the
Water out of Smith Creek at the Junction of the two
forks where this Stake Stand I shall build the dam Some
Six feet high and cary the Water along the South hill to
the Emegrant Road August A.D. 1854 Isaac Roop
Recorded this first day of May A.D. 1856
Isaac Roop Rec

Roop did not fail to consider the practical aspects altogether. As a citizen and merchant of Shasta in the early 1850s, he was intensely aware of the economic opportunities afforded the town by Nobles' Road. The businessmen had financed the exploration of the practical route and had invested time and money in its improvement. Shasta had become the champion of Nobles' Road, and through its voice, the Shasta Courier, had made sure that the rest of the state was aware of the advantages the route possessed. Even if a responsible Shasta citizen had not been over the route himself, he knew all the details of distance, the condition of the trail, and the location of the best watering places.[77]

One of the first spots to become known as an excellent stopping place in the journey was Honey Lake Valley. The first immigrants to reach Shasta over the new route on August 4, 1852[78] reported that they had rested five days in "Honey Lake Valley, at the Eastern foot of the Mountains... owing to the abundance of grass which they there found with which to recruit their stock."[79]

Roop saw that trade with the immigrants along the increasingly well-traveled route would supply him with a livelihood. And Honey Lake Valley was ideally suited for such a plan. Lying at the very edge of the Great Basin, it could not help but appear as a verdant oasis of grass and water to the weary voyager coming from the miles of desert which stretch from the Humboldt to the valley. The rich deep soil which covered the valley floor had been washed down by streams from the steep, timber-covered mountains which rose abruptly at its western edge. Rye and bunch grass grew profusely along the Susan River and the other streams. Game, both large and small, abounded, and the lake served as a haven for many types of waterfowl. On the northeast and far to the southeast, beyond the lake, were low-lying hills which, by their lack of any trees, except scrub juniper, warned of the desert beyond. Here in a valley wilderness, Isaac Roop would work, not only in an effort to recoup his fortune, but to revive his lagging spirits. The valley and the town which grew up about his settlement would come to be his greatest love.

Both Honey Lake and its valley are remnants of ancient Lake Lahontan, which, at its greatest height in 100 A.D., covered 8,422 square miles of the northwestern part of the Great Basin.[80]   At that time, the Honey Lake area was under 325 feet of water.[81]   The western expanse of Lake Lahontan includes the Smoke Creek and Black Rock Desert areas and the valleys of Pyramid, Winnemucca and Honey Lakes.[82] As Lake Lahontan receded, it left even, playa-like lakes, among them Honey Lake. These Great Basin playas have no outlet and are usually very shallow, often evaporating completely in very dry years.[83]The fluctuations are often extreme. When Roop saw Honey Lake in 1853, it was 15 miles long and nine miles wide. By 1859 it was almost dry, but nine years later, it was submerging bordering farm lands. In 1877 its depth was eighteen inches.[84]In 1942, it had a depth of twelve feet,[85]and in 1949 it was a mudhole again.[86]Often it is almost full and presents a beautiful sight to the motorist traveling north on U. S. 395.

Roop stayed in the valley improving his claim until late November, and then returned to Shasta for the winter. He was caught by a snowstorm but happened upon an old trapper's cabin where he was forced to stay for nine days, living on some barley which had been left there.[87]   He spent the winter months concluding the affairs of the estate of Josiah Roop. As administrator of his brother's will, he went to court concerning claims against and debts owed to the estate.[88]

Roop was also preparing to return to Honey Lake Valley. In May 1854, he and a companion, John Hill, started for Honey Lake Valley to see if they could get a wagon load of supplies through the snow. After they got into the mountains, they came upon a prospecting party out from Shasta. The combined group reached Honey Lake Valley on June 6, 1854.[89] The prospectors found little encouragement and left in disgust while Roop and Hill hurried back over the range to gather merchandise and men. As soon as possible, the group started for the valley. Among the men who came with Isaac were Ephraim Roop, one of Isaac's brothers, William McNaull and William Weatherlow.[90] The men immediately began building a log house.

In July, a party under the leadership of Lt. E. G. Beckwith came through the valley exploring Nobles' Road as a possible route for the proposed transcontinental railroad. An entry in his report, dated July 3, 1854, states, "As we entered Honey Lake Valley, we found two brothers by the name of Roop, busily engaged in erecting a loghouse and planting a small field. They had been here but a month."[91] Roop later recorded the building of the house along with his copy of the original land claim.[92]

When the building was finished, Roop opened his trading station.[93] From the first, he kept a house register. It was intended to serve as a count of the emigrant traffic which passed by, but soon the signatures of the travelers were intermingled with the writings of the local citizenry. Verse, comments upon life in the valley and humorous description make it "a source book of the first rank for the study of pioneer life."[94]

On July 4, Roop first recorded the appearance of Indians near his house. The entry for July 14 states, "Second appearance." and is followed by "July 17, 18, 19th with cheaf." This probably refers to Old Winnemucca, the chief of the Paiute tribe which ranged from Pyramid Lake to Honey Lake Valley. Roop had already met with Winnemucca the previous November, just before he returned to Shasta.[95]

The first immigrants reached the valley on July 21.[96] By July 25, 96 men, 7 women and 11 children had passed by. Dozens of travelers signed the register. Since Roop's house was the first station after the Humboldt River, it was a welcome sight to the desert-weary traveler. By August 18, the numbers had swollen to 522 men, 96 women and 51 children.

The entries in the register give a vivid impression of Isaac Roop and the life he and the other settlers led during the first summer of settlement. In addition to selling goods to the travelers, Roop improved his claim, hunted, and searched for possible improvements and short cuts in the road to make it more appealing for travel. Life was not easy for the group working in the wilderness, but the men compensated for this by their humor, of which there are liberal samplings in the register. On August 4, Roop and some others went hunting and recorded the results: "up Smith Creek Roop Walden & Tutt and four dogs Boston, Tiger and two cats all told, two grizzly one antelope and a digger squaw." One of Roop's entries states:

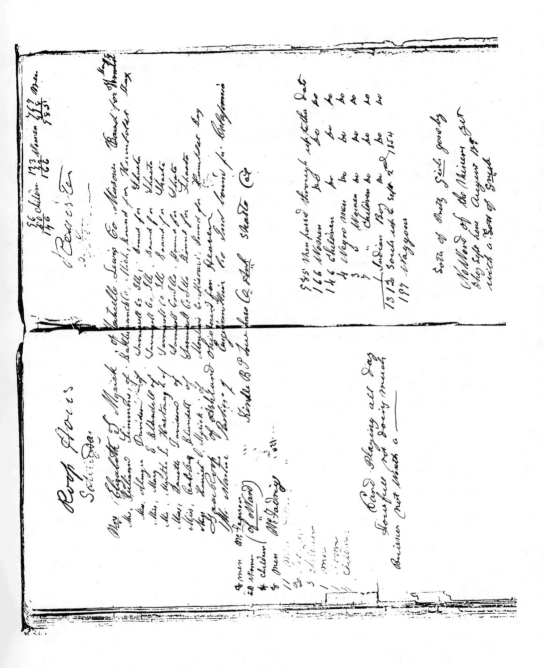

Roop House Register, entries of September 2, 1854

Courtesy of Faye Messinger

> Great works going on today -- washing dishes -- diggin
> ditches -- building reservious wetting down - looking
> for Emigrants (Ladies) non in sight. If you are coming
> why don't you come along...

The ditch mentioned was on what was then called Smith Creek, the present Paiute

Creek, which flows into the Susan River near Roop House. Roop posted a notice

claiming "the privilege to take all the water out of Smith Creek at the junction of the

two forks where the stake stands I shall build a dam some six feet high and carry

the water along the south hill to the emigrant road."[97] Fairfield states that "this

ditch was the beginning of a water system that supplied Susanville with water until

the early '70s."[98]

Later in August, Roop recorded that he "had a hell of a time fighting fire

came very nigh burning up the whole valley."[99] And, on October 1, Roop wrote:

> Start out on an Indian hunt 4 of us Jenkins Wright
> Sunderlin and Myself Don't know when we shall be
> back

Then on October 3,

> Got back tonight Gone 2 days and 2 nights found non
> traveled over the damnedest country that a white men
> ever saw was at Eagle Lake it is some 9 miles from here

These Indians most probably were Pit River Indians who had stolen stock, as Roop

records in other places. They usually came into the valley from their more northern

habitat and harassed the Honey Lake settlers. In mid-October, Roop furnished the

Shasta Courier with the following figures: 3,228 people had passed through the

valley with 510 wagons, 33 spring wagons and about 33.000 cattle, horses and

mules.[100]

October also brought cold and stormy weather, and some of the men

started to leave the valley before snow closed the mountain passes. However, a few

stayed in the Roop House for the winter.[101] Whether Isaac Roop was one of them

has not been agreed upon by historians of the area. One source, giving no reference,

states that when winter set in, "Roop and the larger number of his companions returned to Shasta, while a few stopped in the valley until spring..."[102] Fairfield quotes Roop's daughter, Susan Roop Arnold, a resident of Susanville from 1863, as saying that Isaac and Ephriam Roop stayed in the valley during the winter of 1854-1855.[103] However, the last entry in the Roop House Register for 1854 is dated October 3. It is probable that Isaac left for Shasta shortly after this, for the Shasta Courier of October 21, 1854, in reporting the figures of immigration through Honey Lake Valley, states that they represented the totals furnished by Isaac Roop "up to the time of his departure from his ranch in Honey Lake Valley, a week or more since..."[104] Later, the same paper contained a notice dated November 17, 1854, announcing that Isaac Roop, as administrator of his brother's estate, would make a final settlement in the Probate Court of Shasta County.[105]

On January 29, 1855, Roop, along with 26 of the leading citizens of Shasta, signed a petition to the State Senate Committee on Internal Improvements.[106] The petition was concerned with the perennial interest of Shasta, the improvement of Nobles' Road. The petitioners wished "that a wagon and stage road could be constructed from the Humboldt River to the Immigrant Ferry on the Sacramento River." Isaac Roop was the second to sign, directly under the signature of D. D. Harrill, who had replaced him as postmaster. Undoubtedly, Roop was one of the major promoters of this venture.

The above evidence proves that Isaac Roop was in Shasta during most of the winter of 1854-1855. Although Roop was the first to claim land in the valley and to build a house, he cannot be considered as the first year-round resident. That distinction goes to those men who stayed in Roop's cabin during that winter of 1854-1855.

The year 1855 saw the coming of more settlers. Additional land was claimed. Perhaps the best known newcomer of that year was Peter Lassen. In June, Lassen, with a group of men, came into the valley on a prospecting trip. They had traveled over the mountains from Indian Valley, where Lassen and Isadore Meyerowitz, his companion of the Gold Lake expeditions, had been living since 1851. After prospecting with some good results along the southwestern edge of

Honey Lake Valley, the group returned to Indian Valley.[107] There Lassen gathered supplies and livestock, and in October with Meyerowitz, Joseph Lynch and two others, returned to Honey Lake Valley in order to establish a permanent base of operations. Later in the year, John Duchesne came over from Quincy, and Newton Hamilton and Marion Lawrence (better known as Commanche George) drifted into camp and made an agreement to stay with Lassen. About this time, two of the original party returned to Indian Valley. The six men mentioned above prepared for winter by cutting wild hay for the stock and building the Lassen cabin on Lassen Creek, about four miles south of the Roop House. Here they stayed throughout the winter.[108] In November, Moses Mason claimed land along Smith Creek, adjoining Roop's claim on the northwest corner.[109]

Roop worked in the valley but did not record his activities in the Roop House Register. His only entry contains the announcement of his leaving for Shasta with Hasey on November 6, 1855.[110] He remained in Shasta during the winter. Ephriam Roop, McNaull and William Weatherlow wintered in the Roop House.[111]

The year of 1856 saw the beginning of settlement in earnest. Roop and the others, by their frequent trips back to the older settlements, had made the advantages of their valley known. Lassen and the miners began to have moderate success, and soon more men came over the mountains, chiefly from the diggings on the forks of the Feather River. A few came in from the Carson Valley area far to the southeast.[112]

These newcomers were not greenhorns. Most of them had been around California since the first days of the gold rush and knew the hardships of frontier life. When they drifted into the valley, they were aware of the advantages and disadvantages which life there presented. Even though the valley was on a well-traveled route, it was surrounded by Indians and cut off from aid by the mountains and winter snows on one side and the desert and lack of settlement on the other. Despite the isolation and danger, the settlement gained men who, like Roop, were eager to leave the more populated diggings of California to try their luck in Honey Lake Valley.

Those who claimed land in 1856 included the group which had wintered in the Lassen cabin. These men located in the southern end of Honey Lake Valley or in Elysian Valley, the smaller southern adjunct of Honey Lake Valley.[113] Roop, with Hasey, Mason, Strode and Hollingsworth, arrived at Roop House on April 18, 1856.[114] The next day Roop brought his goods over from Lassen's. The following month Roop recorded his daily activities which included a little prospecting, visiting, work on the house, the building of a hen house and a meeting of the settlers.[115] At this meeting, which took place on April 26, 1856, the settlers created the "Territory of Nataqua,"[116] and Isaac Roop, as Recorder of the territory, began keeping a book of land claims filed with this frontier government. The book contained entries from May 1, 1856, to October 18, 1862, and gave almost a complete record of the settlement of the Honey Lake area.[117] The claims were first posted on the land and then filed with Roop. Some of the claims were located by obvious landmarks, but others read like this:

> Notice. I commence at this stake and run east one mile, thence south one mile, thence west one mile, thence north to the place of the beginning. Claimed by Daniel Reed. The II day of March, 1857.[118]

Often claimants did not occupy or improve their land, and many abandoned their claims. Soon the same land would appear in the claim of another, with no relinquishment by the first claimant recorded.[119]

The winter residents of Roop House were among the first to file their claims. Ephriam Roop claimed land on the south side of Susan River, near Curlew Butte, a landmark southeast of Roop House; William Weatherlow located on the north side of the river about a mile and a half east of Roop's place; and A. G. Hasey and Strode, Roop's travelling companions, located south and east of Roop House. Over 60 claims, some being second filings on abandoned claims, were recorded in 1856.[120] In all, 30,000 acres of land were claimed and recorded that year.[121]

Although many men came into the valley to settle down and work the land, they could not be content. Honey Lake Valley, as all frontier settlements, lacked a vital element -- women. The scarcity of women in the valley became the underlying theme of the <u>Roop House Register</u>.   Roop recorded the passing of the first immigrants on August 8.   Ten days later, one of the parties stopped at Roop's overnight, and Isaac arranged an impromptu dance. Someone wrote:

> Danc Last Night Roop Went out and asked the Girles
> in the house and there Was thirteen Girles

Then on the next day, another train passed by:

> They Benches was crowded with Girls.   Roop was
> fixing Some plan to stop them in this Valley...Charley
> Devol and the Balance of the Boys could not say one
> Word to them nohow (Sugar no go)

Later in the month this sage advice was offered by one resident:

> Girls are very scarce non coming of any amount...It is
> no good for a man to be a lone Verely.   Verely I say
> unto you take unto yourself a wife that your days may be
> long in the land of the Lord thy God gave unto you for
> how can a man live to a good old age if he obey not this
> commandment.

The entry of October 9 contained this wry account of the day's travel:

2 Wagons	1 Indian	3 dogs	50 head Cattle
15 Horses	1 mule	Nary woman	

September 9 was a sad day about the Roop House. The week before, the residents had held a dance with some immigrant ladies in attendance. On this day, they hoped to equal their success. But the record reads:

> 9 Prepperation for a danc. and a sad Disapointment.
> No lady could be find. After a hard search som were
> found but ingaged so they could not come...

The count of the immigration for this year is not complete. Slightly over 100 persons were noted in the register. Although the majority were coming to California, some of the travelers were going in the other direction, "bound for the states."

August 1856

Monday 18 1 1856

Dane Last Night.

Roop Went out and and
asked the girles in the
house and thee Was
thirteen a Girles.

Geo W Bees from Grand Rapids
Kent Co Michigan formerly of
New York City Aug 19th 1856
Tho. I Bowling Front Royal Va

I like frying Meat and A
Sage Rooster Dinner Hat

They benches was crowded with Girls
Roop was fixing Some place to stop
them in this Valley
Jess and Cap Charley Devol and
the Balance of the Boys could not say one
word to them nohow (Sugar no go)

Roop House Register, entries of August 18, 1856

Courtesy of Faye Messinger

Roop House and the Lassen log cabin were the centers of trade and gatherings in the valley. Roop House remained the center of the activity along the immigrant road. However, during this year, some other cabins were built. Weatherlow erected one close to Roop's, and E. Smith built one at a spring about a mile and a half south of Roop's. Others sprung up along the lake itself. In all, nine cabins were erected by the end of this year.[122]

Although Roop and those who followed him into Honey Lake Valley knew they had laid claim to valuable land, they did not know exactly where they were politically. In 1850, California had come into the Union with an eastern boundary defined as starting at a point where latitude 42 degrees and longitude 120 degrees met and then due south to latitude 39 degrees and then southeast in a straight line to a point where longitude 35 degrees crossed the Colorado River.[123] The determination of the eastern boundary caused the greatest fight in the constitutional convention,[124] and the compromise line finally agreed upon was to cause unlimited controversy. To the pioneers living along the eastern Sierra, the well-defined lines on the map became nebulous entities. The uncertainty of the exact geographic position of the town which grew up around Roop's claim was to control its history for the next decade.

The influx of settlers in 1856 created a problem of government, so a meeting was held on April 26, 1856.[125] Twenty of the more stable residents of Honey Lake Valley gathered at the Roop House to form "such laws, rules, and regulations as are deemed necessary and advisable in view of the settlement of said valley."[126] Out of the meeting came the Territory of Nataqua. Beginning with the statement, "Inasmuch as Honey Lake Valley is not within the limits of California," the first section of the constitution declared a new territory:

The boundaries thereof shall be as follows:

> viz., Beginning at a point where the 38 1/2 degree of North Latitude crossed the east line of California; thence east to the 117 degree of West Longitude; thence north to the 42 degree North Latitude; thence running west to the 120 degree West Longitude (N. E. corner of

California); thence south to the beginning; the said
territory to be named <u>Nataqua</u> (i. e. woman).[127]

The name of the territory, the Paiute word for woman, reflected the tenor of the
entries in the <u>Roop House Register</u>.

The territory, 240 miles long and 155 miles wide, took in most of what was
then western Utah.[128] This land was unoccupied except in the southern extremes of
the territory, where about 600 residents of Carson Valley lived. The absurdity of the
whole territorial scheme lay in the fact that the settlers had created a territory in
which they did not reside. In actuality, the western boundary was about 35 miles
east of the Roop House. This fact has caused many writers to make light of the
whole movement.[129]

One penetrating study[130] points out, however, that the formation of the
territory was not the most important part of the document.[131] Those gathered at
Roop House were landowners, and land matters and protection were the main
concern of the meeting. Seven of the 20 sections of the Constitution dealt directly
with land ownership. Each male settler 21 years of age had the right to claim 640
acres of land; any person claiming land had to post a dated notice describing the
land, and then file the claim with the recorder; all claims were to be surveyed within
90 days in the presence of the claimant; and all claims had to be occupied by the
claimant or his substitute.[132]

Section six provided an insight into the nature of Isaac Roop. He saw that
a permanent and unified settlement would be advantageous to all, and therefore he
donated land from his original claim for a townsite. The land surrounding the house
"Roop shall cause to be laid out in said plot, and each settler shall be entitled to one
lot in said plot, provided he caused a building to be placed thereon by the first day of
May, A. D. 1857."[133] This was the beginning of Rooptown, now Susanville.

Six sections of the manifesto provided for public roads radiating from the
Roop House. Another forbade the selling or trading of liquor with the Indians.
Section Nine created an arbitration board to settle all disputes in the valley. The

group concluded the meeting by electing Isaac Roop, Recorder and Peter Lassen, Surveyor.[134]

The work of the settlers bears a close resemblance to the miners' laws which permeate the history of western America.[135] The group saw their needs and wrote a practical and direct document to suit their requirements. In addition, they believed in the justice of a new territory in western Utah. In all likelihood, they did not feel that Nataqua was to be such a permanent establishment. The territory actually was a frontier land club or claim association, created to protect squatters who had no legal government.[136] It lasted about two years, although Roop recorded land claims until 1862.[137]

The first case recorded by Roop under the laws of Nataqua was the estate of Isadore Meyerowitz, the companion of Lassen in most of his activities. Isadore and his squaw wife, who had settled near the shore of Honey Lake, had gone out on the lake in a homemade boat. A wind come up and overturned it, drowning both of them.[138] On July 27, Roop and Lassen were sworn in and George Lathrop was made administrator.[139]

The Board of Arbitration functioned throughout the year, carrying out the enforcement, interpretation and decision-making necessary under the laws. The board kept peace in the valley by meeting quickly whenever a dispute arose. Several cases of claim jumping were arbitrated during the summer.[140]

The publicity which accompanied the formation of the new territory caused a new rush of immigrants to Honey Lake Valley.[141] By the end of 1856, all of the good land in the valley had been claimed.[142]

On August 29, 1856, Isaac Roop left for Shasta.[143] It had been the practice of many of the Honey Lakers to spend the worst of the winter months in the older settlements west of the Sierra. After the winter of 1856-1857, however, Roop and most of the settlers resided only in Honey Lake Valley.[144]

During 1857, the settlement now known as Rooptown, returned to its isolated existence. Except for Indian difficulties, life was peaceful. On June 9, Roop recorded, "the Neighbors Gathered Togather & raised Cut Arnolds House   got

Drunk & retired."[145] The Arnold House was the first hotel and restaurant in
Rooptown and a sign that the town had become permanent.[146] In July of that year,
Roop and McNaull built the first sawmill in the valley. It was located up the Susan
River from Rooptown and depended upon water for power.[147] By August 8, the
count of immigration for the summer stood at 970 men, 305 women and 488
children, with 396 wagons and 19,893 head of cattle.[148]

By April of 1858, Roop had named the town Susanville in honor of his
daughter.[149] More and more settlers came in. Storekeepers A. W. Worm and
Charles Nixon constructed buildings and took over the merchandising business
originally supplied by the Roop House.[150] On March 19, 1859, Isaac Roop
established an unofficial post office to handle the mail which was now regularly
brought over the mountains from Shasta and Quincy.[151]

Isaac Roop, in little over six years, had carried on an active life as a
pioneer. His history during these years is also the history of Honey Lake Valley. As
a settler he had proved successful. His town, established permanently by 1858, still
stands over 100 years later. However, in other fields, Isaac Roop was still obliged to
prove himself. The perennial problems of the Indian menace and political and
geographic uncertainty of Honey Lake Valley were to make his life much more
complex in a short while.

CHAPTER THREE
UNIFYING THE EASTERN SLOPE

From 1856 to 1861, Isaac Roop, as the founder and leader of the Honey Lake settlement, became involved in a series of attempts to create a new territory along the eastern slope of the Sierra Nevada. When the Honey Lake Valley people created their Territory of Nataqua in 1856, they were not acting without precedent. Frontier history contains numerous examples of similar squatter governments and territories. However, the Nataquans did not have to look back to the early days of our national history to find a precedent. Carson Valley, settled less than five years before Roop filed his claim in Honey Lake Valley, was still very much alive and replete with examples of its own.

The Carson Valley community grew up around the station built for trading with the California-bound pioneers in 1849. It was nominally under the control of the government in Salt Lake City. At the time of its founding, the Mormon territory of Deseret was in operation. When this territory was superseded by the Territory of Utah in 1850, Mormon Station, as the Carson Valley settlement became known, passed under its control. Probably neither the territorial officials nor the settlers in the valley were aware of this fact. No one knew where the boundary line which separated California from its eastern neighbor actually lay. This uncertainty was to control the actions of the eastern Sierra citizens for the next decade and a half.

The settlers in Carson Valley were isolated. The imposing Sierra with its severe winter storms was directly at their backs, and between the valley and Salt Lake City lay hundreds of miles of desert inhabited only by Indians. The Carson Valley residents decided to organize a squatter government. The first meeting was on November 12, 1851, at Mormon Station.[152] The organizers agreed to petition Congress for the formation of a distinct territory. Their main concern, as was the case in so many similar attempts, was not the separate territory, but rather the recording of land claims and the preservation of peace and order. The first three meetings of the citizens set up the offices of recorder and surveyor, provided for rules of filing land claims and paying filing fees and for the organization of a civil government to enforce law and maintain order.[153]

In 1852, the California Legislature took cognizance of the Carson Valley settlement and created the County of Pautah, completely outside the boundaries of California. The proposed county was to include much of present western Nevada.[154] It was to begin functioning when Congress transferred the area in question from the Territory of Utah. Congress did not look favorably upon the plan and Pautah County never was organized.

By 1853, the Carson Valley residents had abandoned the territorial aspects of their government and were petitioning California for annexation.[155] The appeal resulted in an attempt to move the California boundary eastward to include the eastern slope of the Sierra. The planned memorial to Congress to effect this was killed in the California Assembly.[156]

Meanwhile, Utah Territory, realizing the value of a Mormon settlement along the base of the Sierra, had created a series of long, narrow counties stretching from the main Utah settlements westward to the California boundary. However, these counties never exercised any control over western Utah.[157] The annexation attempt by California caused the Utah government to create Carson County in western Utah on January 17, 1854.[158] The county extended from the 118th meridian to the elusive California boundary and included the area from Honey Lake on the north to the region below Mono Lake on the south.

Mormon officials were sent to the Carson Valley. The organization of the county was entrusted to Orson Hyde, one of the Twelve Apostles of the church, who was also Probate Judge of the territory's third judicial district.[159] Judge Hyde was not positive that the settlement in which he was to organize Carson County was in Utah Territory. Before he began the organization, he contacted the California authorities in order to establish the exact location of Carson Valley.[160] California, involved in a wagon road survey in the area, then authorized the setting of a point to find if the angle of the state line fell in Carson Valley. The survey of that portion of the boundary was made in 1855 by George Goddard. He found that the angle fell in Lake Tahoe, a few miles west of Carson Valley.[161]

The assumption of control by the Mormons added a new factor to the confused boundary situation. Although the settlers of the valley wanted government, they were not anxious to be controlled by Mormons. The non-Mormons, or Gentiles, who were in a majority in the valley until 1855, became active in trying to get out from under the government which Utah had sent them. The moves by the conflicting parties -- the Gentile settlers, the California authorities and the Utah Territory officials -- became more and more confusing in the next few years.

The Goddard survey findings caused the settlers to again petition California to extend its boundaries to include the eastern slope.[162] The California Assemblymen who advocated a larger state at the expense of Utah Territory used this petition to put a memorial to Congress, through the Legislature, requesting the extension of the eastern boundary of California to the 118th meridian.[163] The memorial was not acted upon by Congress.[164]

For the next two years, the Mormons controlled western Utah. Mormon settlers were sent out from Salt Lake City. The old Mormon Station was surveyed and enlarged. Orson Hyde renamed it Genoa. The majority of the settlers in Carson Valley and the other nearby valleys were now Mormons.[165] However, Mormon rule was not to last for long. It ended abruptly in 1857 when the call was issued from Salt Lake City for all Mormons to return and defend the Church from the oncoming U. S. Army. All the record books, papers and proceedings of the courts were to be returned to Salt Lake immediately.[166]

This was a blow to the Gentiles. They were gratified to see the Mormons leave the area, but their departure caused the government to revert back to the confused situation of 1854. Instead of allowing it to return to a state of neglect, the settlers saw an excellent opportunity to revive the idea of creating a separate territory. Even before the Mormons had left the valley, the remaining settlers called a preliminary meeting on August 3, 1857, to plan for a general convention.[167] The first resolution of this meeting called for a convention of delegates representing all of the western part of Utah to meet on August 8, 1857, in Genoa.[168] This resolution laid the groundwork for the first unified attempt at government by the settlers of the eastern slope.

Enthusiasm must have been high, for in the short time of five days, delegates gathered from a great area. The southern area of Walker River and Walker Valley sent delegates, as did the northernmost valley, Honey Lake. In between these and stretching into the desert, the central area yielded delegates from Carson Valley, Eagle Valley, Hope Valley, Sink of the Humboldt, Willow Town, Twenty-Six Mile Desert and Ragtown.[169]

For the first time, Honey Lake Valley took action in conjunction with the other valleys in the Great Basin. Being isolated from the central cluster of eastern slope valleys by distance, Honey Lake Valley had developed apart from them. Nearly all of Honey Lake Valley's antecedents lay in Shasta and far northern counties of California. Isaac Roop came into the valley directly from Shasta. During his first years there, he supplied his trading station with salable items from Shasta, to which he often returned on business. Most of the first settlers of the valley filtered across the Sierra from the same general area Roop had left. Despite the ties which existed across the mountains, the connection was bound to be weakened. Contacts with settled valleys along the eastern slope diverted the flow of trade southward and eliminated the arduous journey across the mountains.[170] Nearly all the centers of population on the eastern slope in the early years had originated as stations for trade with California-bound travelers. Many of the ranches sprung up to supply food and animals for trade. In every valley, the permanent residents were faced with similar economic situations and political problems and worked under the same geographic and climatic conditions. Unity of attitudes and action was inevitable.

Honey Lake Valley had been developing rapidly during this period. Like their counterparts in Carson Valley, the Honey Lakers lacked government in their area. They did not know whether they were in California or not. If they were, they fell under the jurisdiction of Plumas County, with the county seat, Quincy, over 50 miles to the southwest, in the midst of the Sierra. If they were outside the state, as the advocates of Nataqua nearly always claimed, they were isolated, for Utah had never extended its authority into the valley. The creation of the Territory of Nataqua was the answer for the original settlers led by Isaac Roop and Peter Lassen. This elaborate frontier government was still nominally in effect when the Genoa convention was called. Roop and the Honey Lake leaders undoubtedly realized that Nataqua had served its local purpose and felt no regret at starting on another territorial venture in Genoa. The conditions existing in Utah and the chance to unite with other eastern slope residents for the first time in presenting their case to Congress was too promising an opportunity to pass up.

The convention met.[171] John Reese of Genoa, one of the promoters of the venture, was elected president, and Isaac Roop was made one of the four vice-presidents.[172] The convention appointed a committee to present the business before the meeting. While the committee was working, the convention was addressed by James M. Crane, a journalist from San Francisco. He had been editor of the California Courier in San Francisco and was in Nevada at the time searching for geological specimens to use in a lecture series.[173] Crane was a fluent speaker and, seeing the opportunity afforded him, he fell in with the movement. He addressed the convention and drew the praise of the assembled delegates for his ability and knowledge. They chose him to proceed to Washington and urge territorial status. If successful, he was to become their congressional delegate.[174]

The convention drew up a memorial to Congress asking for the creation of a new territory, including the area from the eastern boundary of California along the 42nd parallel to the 116th meridian, southeast to a point near present day Phoenix, Arizona, south to the Mexican border, and then west to the California line.[175] To prove the need for such a territory, the memorial stated that the people had no protection from the Indians and outlaws and that the Territory of Utah afforded them no government; the isolation due to the winter snows and great distances was also a prime consideration. The distance from Salt Lake City to "the innumerable fertile valleys which lie along the eastern spurs and foot-hills of the Sierra Nevada, where the most of the population of this section reside, is nearly 800 miles, and over this immense space there sweep two deserts."[176] In relation to Honey Lake Valley, the memorial was explicit. Honey Lake Valley "lies east of the Sierra Nevadas, and within the Great Basin, and from this cause the people living in it have not intercourse with the other parts of the State during the rainy season for nearly four months of the year."[177] The memorial concluded with a few supported "facts" to bolster its cause. It stated that there were 7,000 to 8,000 people living in the area under consideration and that over 200 valleys "all alluvial...are the best grazing and agricultural lands on this continent." Two statements were strangely prophetic -- that there were rich deposits of precious minerals throughout the territory and that soon the area would be overrun by new settlers.

Having produced this document containing both fact and fiction, the convention made ready to adjourn. A committee of 27 was appointed to keep the territorial bandwagon moving in the various settlements. Representing Honey Lake Valley on the committee were Roop, Lassen and three others.[178]

While Isaac Roop was in Genoa, important events were occurring in Honey Lake Valley. On August 4, 1857, the Plumas County Board of Supervisors created Honey Lake Township.[179] The Honey Lakers were quick to retaliate against this move toward organization by the California county. In a meeting on August 29,

1857, at the ranch of Manly Thompson, the settlers made their stand clear.[180] They expressed "reasonable doubt" that the valley lay in California and argued that until the survey was run by authorized officials, "no county or counties have the right to extend their jurisdiction over us."[181]   Therefore, the citizens resolved that they "consider the action of the Board of Supervisors of Plumas County an unwarrantable assumption of power."[182]   The document then charged Plumas County officials guilty of usurping power by appointing justices, planning elections and ordering assessment of property in the valley. The settlers further resolved to ask the Plumas County officials to keep the polls closed upon the day of election. They appointed a "Committee of Safety" to correspond with the Plumas officials and "to end meetings when necessary." The citizens also gave their endorsement to the newly planned territory in western Utah.[183] The meeting ended after two final resolutions passed.

> Moved, that the citizens of this valley attend the place of voting on the day of election, and prevent the polls being opened. Carried.   Moved, that a committee of three be appointed to wait on Dr. Fredonyer on of the newly appointed Plumas justices, and politely inform him that the citizens of this valley can dispense with his services. Carried.[184]

The document was signed by 32 citizens. Isaac Roop evidently was not in the valley at this time, but the meeting was recorded in his Nataqua record book.[185]

The results of the meeting were not long in coming. The Marysville Express of about a month later reports the first encounter of the citizens with the Plumas officials.

> ...When the tax collector of Plumas county came among them, they told him they were not in California but in Utah, and when Orson Hyde from Salt Lake visited them they said they lived in California. A portion of the people tried to hold an election there on the day of the last general election, but the rest got double-barreled shotguns, revolvers, and butcher knives and stampeded the whole ballot box establishment, 'horse, foot, and dragoons'[186]

The next important meeting in the valley was held on October 3, 1857.

Isaac Roop called the meeting to order, and the group chose Peter Lassen to preside.[187] A committee composed of Roop, William Cornielson, Jarvis Taylor, William Weatherlow and Mark Haviland retired to report the business. While the committee was meeting, James Crane, not yet departed for Washington and always ready to speak, addressed the group for one hour, reviewing "the policy of the government from 1798 to the present time."[188] The committee reported a number of resolutions which were discussed and adopted. They endorsed the Genoa Convention and memorial, and pledged the support of the Honey Lake settlement in the undertaking. "If any attempt is made by the authorities of California to bring the people of Honey Lake Valley into subjugation before the line can and shall be made,...we will resist all such attempts with all the power we can command."[189] They accused the California authorities of trying "to extend their jurisdiction over us for the purpose of extorting revenue from our people," without trying to defend or protect lives and property.[190] The Shasta Courier, in reporting the meeting, attributed the bellicose attitude to Judge Crane: "any merely mortal man, after being forced to listen an hour to Judge Crane, will be in a fit state of mind to do any desperate deed."[191] Roop, William N. Ormsby of Carson Valley and Martin Smith of Lake Valley were "to bring before the legislature of California a proposition to transfer all of her real or supposed claims to lands lying east of the Sierras to the new territory."[192] The meeting ended with a few "martial airs" by Mr. Harden's band.

Crane left for Washington shortly afterward. The California Legislature aided the cause of the eastern slope residents by passing a resolution favoring territorial status for them because of difficulties in Utah.[193] Governor Weller appended a note of approval to the citizens' memorial and forwarded it to Washington.[194] Crane presented it and awaited action. In a letter to his constituents dated February 18, 1858, he said that the territory bill, with the western boundary fixed as the summit of the Sierra, was sure to be passed soon.[195] Crane urged the settlers to "sow and plant heavy crops of grain and vegetables...for they will bring ready sale at good cash prices to supply the army and the Indians on their reservations."[196]   He also promised the establishment of numerous mail routes throughout the territory.

Crane had good reason to feel confident about the chances for success. This period was one of great antagonism against the Mormons because of the publicity resulting from the Mountain Meadows Massacre of September, 1857. Reduction of the territory controlled by the Mormons was a distinct possibility.   In March, Crane wrote that the territory was certain to be created and that he would leave Washington in May, 1858, with the commissions for the territorial officers.[197] The Committee on Territories in the House of Representatives reported a bill to organize the territory in May.[198]   But this was to be the high point for the Territory of Sierra Nevada.   The representatives of the southern states would have nothing to do with the admission of the territory at that critical time in the slavery controversy.[199]   In addition, the situation in Utah had also changed.   Alfred Cummings had replaced Brigham Young as governor, and the Mormon-related conflicts were subsiding.   Washington did not feel the need for a separate territory at this time.   Judge Crane, very disappointed, returned west and advised the settlers to form a provisional government for their own protection.[200]

While the fate of the territory was being decided in Washington, Isaac Roop was engaged in local Honey Lake affairs.   In February, 1858, he recorded a meeting at which the old land laws of Nataqua were reorganized.   The settlers were to operate on the revised Nataqua government and await the formation of the new territory by Congress.   Meanwhile, they retained the basic form of the old Nataqua system.   A modified settlers' meeting and the same land laws were the foundations for the revised government.[201]

The difficulties with Plumas County had quieted considerably from the year before.   Not being absolutely certain that the valley was in their county, and facing the possibility that the eastern slope would be sliced from California by the new territory, the Plumas officials were waiting to see which way Honey Lake Valley would fall.

After the death of the territory bill, confusion returned to the eastern slope. Governor Cummings of Utah attempted to reorganize the old Carson County. He commissioned John S. Child, Probate Judge and called an election of county officials for October 30, 1858.[202] The election was held, and a bitter contest ensued in many of the races. Most of the returns were thrown out because of illegal voting.[203] As usual, once the election was over, the citizens of Carson Valley paid little attention to the results. The officers had practically no business to transact or duties to perform.[204]

No one seemed to be satisfied with the status quo on the political scene, so in June, 1859, the territorial ball was started rolling again. The citizens called a meeting for June 6, in the town of Carson City which had been laid out the previous year.[205] They divided the Carson County area into precincts to elect delegates to Washington and called a convention to meet at Genoa on July 18 "to count the votes for Delegates, give the successful candidate his credentials and take such other action as the emergency demands."[206] After other preliminary meetings, the convention delegates, elected on July 14, met in Genoa.[207] The sessions lasted for ten days. There were 44 delegates: Honey Lake sent 12, Carson Valley 12, Eagle Valley 12, the Humboldt 4, Long Valley 3 and Walker River 1. Again, Isaac Roop was one of the four vice-presidents of the convention. After some discussion on whether to elect another group to meet as a constitutional convention, the delegates declared their meeting a constitutional convention and set about their business.[208] Since they had received no federal support for a territorial venture, these citizens of western Utah created their own provisional territory to function until Congress saw fit to admit them.

The first document to come out of the Convention was a Declaration of Cause of Separation.[209] It detailed the various abuses the delegates felt had been inflicted by the Mormon government, traced the previous attempt at territorial status, and concluded by saying that "believing in the rectitude of our intentions and believing the time has arrived, we make known and declare our entire and unconditional separation from eastern Utah."[210] With Isaac Roop in the chair, the

Convention adopted the Constitution on July 28, 1859. It provided for a territory stretching from the Oregon line south to the Colorado and Virgin Rivers and spanning the Great Basin from the crest of the Sierra to a line drawn north from the junction of the Virgin and Muddy Rivers to the 42nd degree. The government of the territory was to rest upon a governor, a two house legislature, a secretary of state, a judiciary and other officials.[211]

The Convention had only to canvass the votes of the earlier election for a territorial delegate and its work would be through. After some dispute over the validity of certain votes supposedly cast by immigrants passing by the Humboldt, James M. Crane was named the delegate again, defeating Frederic Dodge, 439 to 378. [212]

The Constitution was to be put to a vote on September 7, 1859, when the territorial officials were to be elected.[213] Isaac Roop and John A. Slater were nominated for governor. The election took place but the board of canvassers who were to ascertain the names of those elected never met. However, J. J. Musser, the president of the Constitutional Convention, certified that the votes were received by him instead and that "a large majority of the votes cast were in favor of the Constitution, and also that Isaac Roop was elected Governor of the said Territory by a large majority."[214] In Genoa and Carson Valley, Roop received 167 votes to 5 for his opponent.[215]

In December, Roop made the 125-mile journey on horseback from Susanville to Genoa to take the oath of office.[216] The winter was severe that year, and he almost froze to death on the way. At Huffaker's in Truckee Meadows, he had to be helped off his horse and carried inside and thawed out before he could continue the journey.[217] On December 13, 1859, Roop was sworn in as Governor of the Provisional Territory of Nevada by F. M. Preston, United States Commissioner, Second Judicial District, Utah Territory.[218]

Here, finally, was what seemed to be the triumph for which Roop and all of the eastern slope citizens had been striving since the early years of the decade. However, the formation of their territory faded into insignificance when put alongside the other happenings in the same area during the latter half of that year, 1859. While the sober-minded settlers were arranging for their elections in June and July leading to the Genoa Convention, the miners along Gold Canyon and Six-Mile Canyon on the slopes of Sun Peak had simultaneously discovered the silver-rich Comstock Lode.[219] By December, when Roop was sworn in, the area's population had doubled. It would have gone much higher had the winter snows not cut off the flow of miners from California until spring.

On December 15, 1859, at a house in Genoa, Roop met for the first time with the Legislature.[220] It was also the last meeting, and for that matter, the last Legislature. The government was paralyzed. The miners who had flocked over the Sierra knew or cared little about a government created by some settlers having no more status than a vigilance committee of their own creation. Again, the efforts of the settlers to provide adequate government suffered a setback. Roop, with the experience of Nataqua behind him, realized that under the changed situation, he could not control such a large area without the support of legislation from Washington. This would be slow in coming because the delegate, Judge Crane, had recently died in Virginia City.[221] As a result, it was necessary to wait until the newly elected delegate, J. J. Musser, could reach Washington and move Congress to action. Therefore, in his message to the Legislature, Roop sensibly proposed that, despite the justice and effectiveness of the separation from Utah Territory, the "organization of the provisional government, would, at the present time, be impolitic."[222]

> At that time we were compelled to assemble, in our sovereign capacity, to endeavor to rid ourselves of the Theocratic rule of Mormonism, we had no protection for life, limb, or property. We had in vain petitioned Congress for relief against the unjust and illegal attempts of Mormons to force upon us laws and customs obnoxious to every American. We had no courts, no county organizations, save those controlled by the sworn satellites of the Salt Lake oligarchy. Our political rights were entirely at the will of a certain clique composed of those who were opposed to the first principle of our constitution, freedom of the ballot-box.[223]

Believing it "to be the wish of the people still to rely upon the sense of justice of Congress" to "relieve the citizens of the evils to which they have been subjected," Roop adjourned the legislature until the first Monday in July, 1860.[224]

The legislature never met again. "Governor" Roop was the only official ever called upon to perform any duties. These duties were in connection with the turbulent Indian situation which finally erupted into a full-scale war early in 1860.

From the time of his first claim in Honey Lake Valley, Isaac Roop had been dealing with the Indians. He had placed his original claim in a valley which was the traditional hunting grounds of six Indian tribes. They were the Modoc, Achomawi (Pit River Indians), Atsugewi (Hat Creek Indians), Northeastern Maidu, Northern Paiute and Washo.[225] The most frequent visitors were the Pit Rivers, Paiutes and Washos.

In contrast to the bitter conflict between the Indians and whites in much of northern California, fairly friendly relations were maintained in Honey Lake Valley during the early years of settlement. This was due chiefly to the efforts of Peter Lassen and Isaac Roop. As early as 1853, Roop had talked to Old Winnemucca, the chief of the Paiutes who ranged from Honey Lake Valley to Pyramid Lake.[226]

In 1856, Old Winnemucca and the settlers of Honey Lake Valley, led by Roop and Lassen, made a treaty. They agreed that if any Indian molested or stole from the whites, a complaint to Winnemucca would be made before the whites took revenge. In turn, Winnemucca would report any wrongs done to his people by the whites, who would then take action.[227] This treaty was observed by most of the people on both sides for a number of years. The Paiutes moved freely in the valley and bartered game and pelts for food and clothing.[228]

The greatest harassment for the Honey Lakers came from the Pit River Indians. The settlers were able to make treaties with this tribe. From the first years, small parties of Pit River Indians would raid the settlements and drive off stock. In October 1857, when some cattle were stolen, the citizens of the valley decided to send an expedition north to chastise the Pits.[229]

Since the Honey Lake area had little or no protection by official government forces, all of the Indian fighting was handled by the settlers themselves. William Weatherlow, who had a reputation as an Indian fighter back in his Shasta days in 1852,[230] willingly became the leader of the volunteer militia, the "Honey Lake Rangers." On this 1857 expedition, Winnemucca and some of his Paiute warriors joined in the search, for the Pit River Indians were their common enemy. Traveling north in California, they were unable to find the elusive, fast moving Indians, but they did destroy some of their lodgings.[231] Returning to Honey Lake Valley, the party found that Washos had come into the southern end of the valley and were raiding ranches. A battle ensued, in which about 10 Indians were killed.[232] Because of so much activity, a major Indian scare resulted. In a letter to the Governor of California from "Honey Lake Valley, Plumas County, State of California," Isaac Roop, M. C. Lake and 45 others appealed for arms.[233]

This petition shows the adaptability of the pioneers. Only two weeks before, many of the same people, including Isaac Roop, had held a settlers' meeting where they approved the Genoa Convention and reaffirmed the stand against California in general and Plumas County in particular. In this instance, the call for help resulted in aid from the state arsenal and a company of men from Sierra Valley.[234] These actions occurred over the strenuous objections of the California press, which had reported the separatist meetings of the last month and could not see why aid should be rendered to areas which considered themselves outside the state.[235]

During the winter of 1857-1858, Roop and Lassen were in communication with the Superintendent of Indian Affairs for California.[236] On January 5, 1858, Roop, Lassen and J. Williams, as sub-agents of the California Superintendent, reaffirmed their earlier treaty with Winnemucca.[237] In a preliminary meeting and at the signing of the treaty, they furnished a total of 90 pairs of overalls, 40 blankets, 82 military jackets and assorted buttons, combs, needles, thread and cloth. On July 18, 1858, they made a similar delivery.[238]

Although the Paiute tribe was still peaceable, the Washos and the Pit River Indians continued to commit depredations. The spring of 1858 was a busy one for Captain Weatherlow, who led nearly all of the Indian tracking. In a letter of April 22, 1858, Isaac Roop told of Weatherlow leading the citizens in two skirmishes within a week.[239] The first was to the south against some Washos who had stolen or killed 30 cattle within six weeks. On this expedition, Weatherlow managed to capture two Indians single-handedly, but needed help from a fellow citizen when they turned on him with a gun. The Honey Lakers managed to kill both Indians.[240] Within a week Weatherlow, leading a party of 15, was traveling north on the trail of Pit River Indians who had also stolen cattle. In his communication, Roop objects strenuously to the lack of military aid from the settled areas.[241]

In May, a group of Honey Lakers were on the trail of some Pit River Indians again. They traveled as far north as Goose Lake on the Oregon line. There they came upon a Mormon party which another band of Pit River Indians were about to capture. In a major battle, the Honey Lakers drove off the Indians, killing over 20.[242] The Pit River Indians remained hostile throughout the spring. About this time, Roop and Lassen wrote a letter to California Indian Superintendent Henley, the only person who had ever sent aid, asking him to recommend the sending of troops to Honey Lake Valley for protection against the Indians.[243] Nothing was done.

In early 1859, there was little trouble with the Indians in the valley itself, but in April, Peter Lassen and Edward Clapper were reportedly killed by Indians while looking for lost silver mines on the Black Rock Desert in Nevada.[244] A certain amount of mystery surrounds the deaths, for the circumstances were unusual, and there was only one white witness. Although Lassen had been friendly with the Paiutes for years, his death appeared to have come at the hands of a renegade band of that tribe,[245] but no one really knows for sure.

The usually friendly Paiutes became antagonistic.[246] Animosities reached a peak in the first month of 1860. Indians killed Dexter Demming, a rancher who lived a few miles south of Honey Lake Valley. This resulted in a petition to

Governor Roop from the Honey Lake people on January 15, 1860. The letter, signed by nearly 100 people, urged Roop to call out the military forces under his command. Since the territory was not organized, this meant the "Honey Lake Rangers." The "Rangers" tracked the Indians in the snow, found they were renegade Paiutes, and recovered some of Demming's belongings.[247]

Roop, acting as governor, appointed Weatherlow and I. J. Harvey to visit Winnemucca.[248] In the subsequent report, Weatherlow said that Winnemucca acknowledged the citizens of Honey Lake were justified in visiting under the terms of their previous treaties, but he refused to search out Demming's killers. In addition, he demanded $16,000 for the land in Honey Lake Valley.[249] Upon receiving the report of his commissioners, Roop wrote to General Clark, commander of the Department of the Pacific of the U. S. Army.[250] He described the situation in the Honey Lake and the eastern slope area. He felt that all evidence pointed to the Paiutes as the ones responsible for the depredations. He recounted the affairs since the murder of Demming and asked for a company of dragoons to come to the settlers' aid.[251] In all, he attributed nine murders, including that of Lassen, to the Paiutes in the prior few months. Roop received no response from General Clark. The presence of troops, as requested, could have had a calming effect on the Paiutes the following May when the Pyramid Lake War took place.

Roop had done about all that was possible considering the lack of any organized government and no authority over a militia. The Pyramid Lake War, which broke out on May 12, 1860, was the result of the irresponsible actions of the whites and the retaliation of the Paiutes. In the subsequent fighting, the Honey Lake citizens had little to do. Weatherlow was on patrol between Pyramid Lake and Honey Lake but missed the battle of Pyramid Lake, in which the Indians slaughtered nearly fifty whites.[252] For a time, Honey Lake was vulnerable to attack, but in August, 1860, a detachment of U. S. Road Survey troops under Colonel Lander came into the valley, thus further securing it.[253] Lander and Weatherlow went out on a joint expedition. Soon after, Young Winnemucca talked with Colonel Lander and then made a treaty with Roop in Susanville in September.[254]

With the attempts to prevent the Indian hostilities from becoming a full scale war, Roop ended his activity as Provisional Governor. The eastern slope had completely changed during the time he was in office. The increase in population and great wealth of the mines brought a new type of life to western Utah. It also brought the attention of Washington. The pleas for a separate territory now had substance. The long sought dream became a reality when the Territory of Nevada came into being on March 2, 1861.[255] The law creating the territory stipulated that the western boundary run along the Sierra summit, provided that the area between the summit and the line of 120 degrees, which lay somewhere east, not be included in Nevada "until California assents to the same by an act irrevocable without the consent of the United States."[256] Isaac Roop and most of the Honey Lakers felt that, in all justice, the summit line would become the western boundary, and Honey Lake Valley would finally become united with the eastern slope. They hoped to stay there for a long, long time.

CHAPTER FOUR
ROOP COUNTY VS. PLUMAS COUNTY

James W. Nye, the first governor of the newly created Territory of Nevada, arrived in Carson City on the evening of July 8, 1861.[257] His first official act concerned the organizing of the territory. Congress, by providing that the western boundary be either the 120th parallel or the summit of the Sierra with the consent of California, had actually created a "floating boundary line."[258] Nevada preferred the summit line, but to insure legality, Governor Nye would have had to defer organization of the strip from 120 degrees to the summit until action by the California Legislature. Governor Nye did not wait for action from California. In proclamations of July 11 and July 24, he organized the territory and provided for districting on the widest limits, including the disputed areas of Honey Lake Valley to the north and Esmeralda or Mono to the south.[259] Honey Lake Valley became part of the Ninth or Pyramid District, which stretched from Long Valley past "Beckworth Road," Bird's Ranch, Fuller's Ranch and Richmond to Susanville. The latter was to be the polling place for the fifth precinct.[260] The governor also called for a census to prepare for the election of the "legislative assembly" and a congressional delegate.

In the absence of any officials to carry out the project, Henry De Groot received the appointment.[261] On August 5, he submitted his report to Governor Nye.[262] The total population of 16,737 included 1,073 in the Pyramid District. Susanville itself had 274 residents.[263]

The election, set for and held on August 31, yielded a total vote of 5,291.[264] John Cradlebaugh, who had been Utah District Judge for the area the previous year, was elected to represent the territory in Congress. Fifteen men were elected to the lower house (the Assembly), and eight were chosen for the upper house (the Council). District Eight chose no councilman. The Pyramid District voters gave 62 of the 68 votes cast for councilman to Isaac Roop.[265] John C. Wright was elected to represent the district in the lower house but never took his seat. In a proclamation of September 10, Governor Nye declared the election results official, and the members of the legislative Assembly elected. He set October 1 for the first meeting of that body.[266]

The first Territorial Legislature was to meet in Carson City, which Governor Nye had declared the temporary capital. The Territorial Secretary, Orion Clemens, was delegated the job of finding a suitable meeting place.[267] The search was a failure until Abram Curry, an early settler, volunteered the free use of his Warm Springs Hotel, two miles from Carson City. The hotel was a two-story stone building, one of the few in the valley. The bottom floor contained the Curry residence and a public dining room and bar. The upper floor was one large room where travelers could bunk on the floor. The large room became the meeting place for the Territorial Legislature. Orion Clemens bought some cloth and divided the room into four sections: one for the Council, one for the House and two small rooms where committees could retire for "privacy."[268]

The "Eagle Valley Railroad," which Curry had built, traversed the alkali plain from Carson City to the hotel. The munificent Curry allowed the legislators to ride free of charge.   The Sacramento Union correspondent who covered the proceedings of the Legislature described the line as follows:

> It runs or rather trots from Carson City across the Eagle
> Valley a distance of a mile and three-quarters (more or
> less) to Curry's Hot Springs Hotel, that is not to say, to
> the Provisional Capital of Nevada Territory. The rolling
> stock consists of a platform car, which carries freight
> from Curry's stone quarry to Carson, and a windowless
> passenger car of primitive construction. Two mules act
> in the capacity of locomotives. Into this car the
> assembled wisdom of the legislature is transported to
> Curry's Hotel and at night to be carted back again. The
> car has not springs, and the members think their daily
> rides afford excellent exercise for the dyspeptic.[269]

The Legislature began its session at the appointed time. Despite the variety and frequency of origin of governments for the eastern slope area, there was no working system of law which the Legislature could take as a basis for the territorial code. They were forced to organize the government from the bottom up, establishing law, organizing departments and passing legislation to meet the wants of the population.[270]

After the preliminary ceremonies were completed, Governor Nye delivered his message, and the two houses began their work.[271] It soon became apparent that one of the leading figures in the Assembly was William M. Stewart, later a long-time senator from Nevada. He introduced a number of significant bills, beginning with one establishing the common law.[272]

Isaac Roop did not attend the first week of the session. He arrived on October 7.[273] When he appeared, Mr. J. W. Pugh, the representative from Carson Valley, called the attention of the Council to the presence of "Governor" Roop, as he had become known. Mr. J. L. Van Bokkelen of Virginia City, the presiding officer, somewhat jokingly said that, so far as he was concerned, the territory had but one governor, and his name was Nye. Mr. Pugh replied, "Well, Mister Roop, then."[274] After this exchange, Chief Justice Turner swore in Roop as a member of the Council.[275] Within a week, Roop introduced his first bill, entitled "An Act to Restrict Herding of Sheep, Cattle, Mules, Jacks, Jennets, Goats or Hogs."[276] This bill is an accurate reflection of the interests of the agricultural area which Roop represented.[277] On October 21, Roop introduced a bill which was to take up a great deal of his time during the session. The bill prohibited the cohabitation or marriage of whites and Negroes, Mulattoes, Chinese or Indians.[278] The bill ran into difficulties, most of which concerned technicalities, however, some members of the Assembly wished to delete Negroes from the prohibition. Roop said he did not like the deletion, but would compromise in order to get the other prohibitions passed.[279] Another member said the House proposal "smacked of Abolitionism" and he would have no part of it. Mr. Stewart supported the original idea but had accepted the compromise in conference committee as the only way of settling the difference of the two branches on the question. He and Roop thought that even the revised form would tend to remove one great cause of most of the Indian difficulties.[280] In the end, all the prohibitions proposed by Roop were incorporated into the law. Punishment for violations was to be from $100 to $500 or imprisonment in the county jail from one to six months.[281]

Roop also introduced other bills relating to the civil and criminal law. Among these was one regulating the "sale of spirituous Liquors" and another defining the duties of judges and clerks of the probate courts.[282]

The Legislature has been immortalized by Mark Twain for its special interest in private legislation, especially toll roads. In Roughing It, the humorist describes one aspect of this legislation in a well-known paragraph:

> The legislature sat sixty days, and passed private toll-road franchises all the time. When they adjourned it was estimated that every citizen owned about three franchises, and it was believed that unless Congress gave the Territory another degree of longitude there would not be room enough to accommodate the toll-roads. The ends of them were hanging over the boundary line everywhere like a fringe.[283]

Actually only eight toll-road bills were introduced in this session,[284] but there was an abundance of private legislation. Roop did not introduce any toll-road measures, but he entered into the private legislation competition by introducing bills to incorporate the Carson City and Humboldt Railroad Companies, the Humboldt River Ferry

Company and the Virginia City Water Company.[285] The ferry venture was anticipated by Roop's brother, Ephriam, William Weatherlow and other Honey Lakers. Roop was also connected with the business affairs of Abram Curry, the owner of the legislative hall. Curry had not offered the use of his hotel to the Legislature for purely patriotic reasons. He had previously made an agreement with William M. Stewart to insure the placing of the Capitol in Carson City so the building could be sold to the territory for public use, probably as the prison.[286] The plan first reached the Legislature in an announcement by Isaac Roop, who gave notice of the introduction of a bill providing for the purchase of the building and grounds for the territorial prison and hospital.[287] Nothing was done this session, but finally, in 1864, the territory bought the property from Curry. The State Prison stands on the site today.[288]

One of Roop's special interests was Council Bill No. 31. Entitled "An Act Relating to Wild Game and Fish," this measure was an early attempt at conservation of the wildlife which abounded in Honey Lake Valley and throughout the area.[289] As enacted into law, it limited hunting seasons and protected birds, fish, deer, antelope, elk and mountain sheep.[290]

The major issues of the session centered around taxation of mining interests, exclusion of out-of-state capitalists, the location of the state capital and the boundary question. Since Honey Lake Valley was a rural area far from the center of population and contained very few mining interests, Roop was not a leader in the fight over the first three of these centers of interest. However, he took an active part, expressing his own views in debate and serving on conference committees, often as chairman of the Committee of the Whole, where most of the legislative work was actually accomplished.

An analysis of the records of the Legislature reveals that Roop came to the session prepared with certain measures such as the ones on marriage and conservation. As he took part, be broadened his interests and contributed to measures far afield from local interest. One such resolution got him into difficulty with Councilman Stewart. Roop introduced a bill providing for the appointment of a commissioner to a world's fair in Great Britain. This brought Councilman Stewart to his feet, protesting that Great Britain had treated our country shabbily and was interfering in the conflict between the North and South. He felt that money should not be wasted on such a venture. Roop replied, complimenting Mr. Stewart's eloquence. He even compared the denunciations of Great Britain to some of the efforts of Patrick Henry. He felt that the nation's rights should be upheld with the sword whenever necessary, but meanwhile they had better send a commissioner to the Fair. The expense was not too great, and the goodwill engendered by the act would return a hundred fold. The resolution passed the Council.[291]

Of special interest to historians was a measure passed on the last day of the session. It provided that "Isaac Roop and others be requested to collect as many of the old records connected with the early history, and also with the Provisional Government of Nevada Territory...for filling in the archives of the Territory."[292]

Another major interest of the session was the proposal of various routes for the transcontinental railroad. On October 21, 1861, Leland Stanford, then governor-elect of California, Collis P. Huntington and Charles Crocker arrived in Carson City to further their railroad venture.[293] They hoped their presence would insure the passage of a bill granting them the continuance of their route across the territory. The Legislature balked at the pressure put upon them. When the bill was introduced, they argued a number of provisions, including the exact location, size of the right-of-way, the possibility of a bank charter being interpreted from the wording of one clause and other provisions. The bill was defeated at first, much to the disgust of the eminent visitors from California. After they had departed, the bill was reconsidered and passed.[294]

The territorial status of Nevada afforded new impetus to the settlement of the perennial boundary question. The "floating" eastern boundary described in the Organic Act actually supported the contentions of men such as Isaac Roop, who wanted all of the eastern Sierra united. Now that they had the voice of an officially recognized government, their hopes of success were high. The Legislature provided for immediate action on the boundary. They considered a concurrent resolution for the election of two boundary commissioners to accompany Governor Nye to the next Legislature of California, to urge the ceding of the portion of land mentioned in the Nevada Organic Act.[295] The resolution passed,[296] and on November 27, the two houses met jointly to elect the commissioners. The first ballot yielded 16 votes for Isaac Roop, 13 for R. M. Ford for the House, 8 for Mr. Mills of the House and 5 for Hannah of the Council.[297] Roop and Ford were declared elected.[298]

With their work completed, the Legislature held its last session on November 29, 1861. The final day was a combination of last-minute business and horseplay. Roop was not above diversions and contributed his part to the levity by offering a resolution arranging "for a military salute over the graves of sundry murdered bills."[299] The chairman declared the resolution out of order. Roop's jovial nature was well known. The best told account of Roop's willingness to participate in the practical joking of the frontier is recorded by Mark Twain.[300]

Despite Twain's humorous estimate that "the first legislature levied taxes to the amount of thirty or forty thousand dollars and ordered expenditures to the extent of about a million,"[301] the Legislature did its job in a conservative manner. The difficulty which arose, however, was the necessity of keeping the rough and unstable population up to the "discreet and moral" standards which the Legislature had set.[302]

In March, 1862, Isaac Roop, R. M. Ford and Governor Nye, as commissioners of the Legislature of Nevada Territory, made the trip to California for the meeting of the Legislature. The weather of the spring was severe, and flooding occurred throughout California. The Sacramento and American Rivers flooded Sacramento, and the legislators were forced to make their trips to and from the capital by boat. After a few days of this, the Legislature moved to San Francisco for the remainder of the session.[303] On March 11, 1861, the Nevada commissioners presented the memorial to Governor Stanford, who should have been expecting it.[304] When Stanford had been in Carson City the preceding fall, various Nevada politicians, including Roop, had approached him to determine his own and California's attitude toward the cession of the eastern Sierra area. When Governor-Elect and Governor Nye came to the legislative chambers, it was Roop who made the resolution offering them "seats within the bar" and escorted them to the places of honor.[305] After discussion in Carson City, Stanford was reputed to be agreeable to cession of the area by the California Legislature, if there were no constitutional objections.[306]

Commissioners Roop, Ford and Nye presented themselves to the Legislature which, by concurrent resolution, scheduled a joint meeting on the evening of March 21, 1862.[307] R. M. Ford began the presentation by reading the memorial of the Nevada Legislature, setting forth the advantages of the Sierra as a permanent boundary. Then Isaac Roop, introduced as the Ex-Governor of the Provisional Territory of Nevada, took the floor. Addressing the meeting "in a plain, practical manner,"[308] he first considered the comparative value of the land in question to California and Nevada. What was worth little to California meant a great deal to Nevada. He traced the summit line and the areas in each of the California counties which would be affected. He pointed out that aside from Mono and Plumas counties, no areas of population would be involved in the proposed cession. All of the economic and social ties of his home area were with Nevada, chiefly because of the great mountain barrier which blocked relations with California many months of the year. He stressed that isolation from the main part of the state and felt, despite the payment of taxes, the region received no benefits from California. The boundary line had been laid down by Jehovah himself, Roop said, and all the commissioners asked was that the California Legislature endorse it. He unrolled a petition from the Mono citizens asking for the cession. He recognized that the line, as set within the last two years, probably put Honey Lake Valley west of the 120th meridian. However, even this line was in doubt. Roop believed a survey of the present line would entail more expense than all the revenue California could collect from the area for the next 50 years. He concluded by thanking the Legislature for hearing the plea and took his seat admist a round of applause.[309]

Roop was followed by Governor Nye. Nye, an impressive and experienced speaker, recounted some of Roop's arguments and added others of his own. He appealed to the natural line of the Sierras and cited the debate in Congress over the creation of the Nevada Territory, which he had attended. He assured the legislators that any mineral wealth found in the area would flow to San Francisco whether the land were in Nevada or not. He took into account the reticence of legislators to give away part of their constituencies, but since Congress had approved of the cession by the Nevada Organic Act, the decision was now up to this body. Since California and Nevada had both origin and interest in mining, they should work together and help each other, he argued. In this case, he said, the land in question was of little value to the vast state of California, with its miles of seacoast and valleys. He concluded by noting the similarities of the two states. He paid tribute to California as the "mother of the West" and concluded by saying that Nevada would be glad to help California at any time.[310]

Following the formal presentations of their requests, the Commissioners stayed in San Francisco to follow the course of actions resulting from them. Certainly they contacted the important legislative members and the representatives of the counties in question. Governor Nye, as chairman of the Commission, appeared before the Judiciary Committee, to which the matter had been referred. Although some committee members felt that the Legislature should make the cession "as a matter of expediency,"[311] there seemed to be constitutional objections. This became the pattern for the remainder of the legislative session. Most of the legislators who said they favored the cession also expressed doubt about the ability of the Legislature to cede the land without an amendment to the constitution of the state.[312] Nye and Roop called attention to Article IV, section 3 of the Constitution of the United States, which gives the power to the legislatures of the states to change their boundaries, with the consent of Congress. They applied this to the present situation and argued that only the consent of the California Legislature was needed to fulfill the constitutional requirements.[313] The bill "to cede certain territory of the State of California to the Territory of Nevada" was introduced and referred to committee.[314] Roop, Nye and Ford remained in San Francisco for six weeks,[315] but their efforts were to no avail. A number of legislators opposed the measure either on the grounds of unconstitutionality or merely because they did not want to give away a slice of California. The bill failed.[316]

During the period from Nataqua to the organization of Nevada Territory, Honey Lake Valley had not been entirely neglected by the agencies of the California government. As soon as there was population enough to warrant action, Plumas County officials, although doubtful, began to exercise what they considered rightful jurisdiction. They organized Honey Lake Township on August 4, 1857,[317] during the same week Isaac Roop was in Genoa, aiding in the first eastern slope attempt at territorial status. As related in the previous chapter, the Honey Lakers wanted no part of Plumas County and in the same month expressed grave doubts that the valley was in California. When the Indian troubles occurred that year, they quickly resolved their doubts and decided they were in California. Then, after conditions returned to normal, they considered their geographic position to be in doubt again. As detailed before, the Honey Lakers stampeded the Plumas attempt for a Honey Lake Township election and revived Nataqua to await the time when Congress would approve the territory proposed in Genoa.

While the Nataquans were creating their territory, the California Legislature turned to a north-south struggle within the state and attempted to divide California into three smaller states. The plan failed, and the original boundaries of 1850 seemed secure. The publicity arising from the attempted division of California and the creation of Nataqua brought renewed interest in the eastern boundary line. The Legislature moved to have it surveyed to insure the legal status of such a boundary. The Legislature also wanted to eliminate the avoidance of tax payments which had created so much news. The Legislature first asked Congress to finance the survey.[318] They received no response.

Meanwhile, a California road survey party, under Kirk, ran an unofficial line north from Lake Tahoe and found that Honey Lake Valley lay almost entirely west of the line.[319] This did not slow the activities of the advocates of a new territory. California then suggested that the state and federal government handle the survey jointly. They recommended this plan yearly from 1858 to 1860.[320] Finally, in 1860, the Legislature determined to mark the boundary itself, and authorized a survey.[321] Later the same year, the California Legislature learned that Congress had finally authorized $55,000 for a survey of the line between California and the territories to the east.[322] California, happy that the line would finally be set, appointed a commissioner to work with the federal officers.[323] Surveyors were in the field by the fall of 1860. For some reason, the whole venture was mismanaged, and by April, 1861, when the work was suspended for lack of funds, only the southern point, where the 35th parallel crossed the Colorado River, was fixed.[324] Maury, the head of the federal party, in apparent attempt to save face, fixed the Lake Tahoe vertex and the northern point on his own time. He then reported that the only tasks remaining were computations and running of the line, which any surveyor could do.[325] As one writer states, this "was a masterpiece in understatement, revealed by later surveys."[326] Had the work been completed, many of the boundary-related difficulties of the succeeding three years in Honey Lake Valley would not have occurred. As it was, California remained without exact knowledge of its eastern boundary.

In Honey Lake Valley itself, the conflict between Plumas and the valley residents had quieted a great deal. The Plumas County sheriff would come over the mountains each fall from the county seat in Quincy to collect taxes. A few of the valley residents would pay, but most would not.[327] Quite often the residents would hold off the sheriff with a gun. On one occasion, the Plumas authorities approached the ranch of "Rough" Elliott, one of the first residents of the valley and a staunch Nataquan. He had refused to pay taxes to Plumas County from the start, and as a result, they intended to take some of his stock in payment. Elliott was not at home, but his wife went out with a shotgun and stood off the intruders, who finally left empty-handed. As one source states, there "was not danger of her getting hurt, for at that time women were very scarce and more valuable then horses, cattle, or taxes."[328]

Eventually some of the valley residents began to weaken in their attitude toward Plumas County. Many of the newcomers to the area, who had not gone through the formative years of the settlement, cared only for order, from whatever governmental agency. Since Plumas County was the most stable, some were ready to accept law from that direction.[329] In November, 1860, Plumas County made a big step forward by managing to hold an election in the valley for justice of the peace. For the next two years, Plumas justices held regular court.[330] The years 1860 to 1861 also saw some of the valley residents journey to Quincy and register their land claims, the first Honey Lake Valley land to be registered anywhere but in Roop's Record Book.[331] Although the hard core of resistance to Plumas had not disappeared, a period of relative political stability prevailed.

The gradual attraction of Roop's settlement into the orbit of the Plumas government stopped suddenly with the creation of Nevada Territory. To Honey Lake Valley, Nevada was a long sought and compatible entity. When Governor Nye of Nevada organized the territory on its widest limits, he knew that Honey Lake must certainly lie west of the 120th meridian. But he and everyone else also knew that the factors of geography, commerce and allegiance put it in the Great Basin.

The provisions of the Nevada Organic Act, already explained, changed the whole boundary picture. In the Honey Lake area, the years of conflict had been concerned with the exact location of the 120th meridian. By this time, 1861, it had unofficially been determined and was accepted by a few. Now the addition of a second line, the summit of the Sierra, provided a new setting for conflict. To the south, along the oblique line running from the intersection of the Colorado River and the 35th parallel, the same confusion existed.[332] The booming Esmeralda mining district was the sought-after prize in that area.

On November 25, 1861, the first Territorial Legislature, in which Isaac Roop took such a large part, created nine counties in Nevada Territory.[333] The northwestern-most of these was Lake County. Its boundary on the north was Oregon, on the east a range of hills just east of the Truckee River, on the south an east-west line running through the mouth of the Truckee River at Pyramid Lake, and on the west the summit of the Sierra.[334] The Legislature appointed three commissioners in each county to provide for an election and handle the other details of county organization. The commissioners for Lake County were William Weatherlow, William Hill Naileigh, and Daniel Murray.[335] At the insistence of Isaac Roop, the Legislature included Lake County in the First Judicial District along with Storey and Washoe counties.[336]

The Lake County commissioners did not provide for the election as instructed, and it remained unorganized.[337] Despite the lack of organization, the county did hold elections on September 3, 1861. A full slate of officers took their position. Among them were the sheriff, William Hill Naileigh, and a clerk, recorder, treasurer, assessor, collector, surveyor and school superintendent.[338] The citizens also chose a representative in the lower house of the Legislature to replace John C. Wright, who had not taken his seat. The man elected, C. Adams, also failed to take his seat, and so Isaac Roop, whose two-year term in the Council had not expired, remained the only member of the Legislature from that area.[339] Plumas County held elections for justice of the peace on the same day as their Nevada counterparts. The polling place in Janesville, a few miles south of Susanville, was Blanchard's store, the voters of Plumas County going to one corner of the room and the Lake County voters to another.[340]

When the Second Territorial Legislature met in the fall of 1862, it was determined to fully organize the county, and insure the jurisdiction of Nevada.[341] On December 2, 1862, the Legislature changed the name of the county. In recognition of the years of effort Isaac Roop expended in the furtherance of the idea of an eastern slope territory and his work as a representative of one of its districts, they renamed it Roop County.[342]

Following this action, the Governor, on December 14 and 15, issued commissions to all the county officers who had been elected in September. At the same time, he also commissioned John S. Ward to serve as Probate Judge.[343] The Legislature completed the action by ordering a special term of the District Court to be held in Roop County in January, 1863.[344]

At the appointed time, Gordon Mott, judge of the First District Court of Nevada Territory, appeared in Susanville. He opened court and swore in the Roop

County officials. This move, completing the cast of characters, was the last of many which set the stage for conflict. Honey Lake Valley, struggling for recognition and government in the 1850s, now had two well-organized and functioning governments. The climax of the confusion and defiance of the last decade had come.

The conflict, dubbed the Sagebrush War, occurred in Susanville in February, 1863. It is perhaps the best known aspect of the valley's history. Both historians and popular writers have examined it in detail.[345]

Roop County Judge John S. Ward made the first move. On January 20, 1863, shortly after he was sworn in, Ward issued an injunction against William J. Young, Plumas Justice of the Peace for Honey Lake Township.[346] Young, who lived and held court in Susanville, ignored the injunction and continued to operate. Ward had him arrested and fined him $100 for contempt of the Roop County court. This brought action from E. T. Hogan, Plumas County judge in Quincy. He issued warrants for the arrest of the Roop County officials, Judge Ward and his sheriff, William Hill Naileigh.[347] The Plumas sheriff, E. H. Pierce, and his deputy, James D. Byers, arrived in Susanville on February 6. Much to his surprise, he was met by William K. Parkinson, deputy sheriff of Roop County, with an injunction from Judge Ward restraining him and all Plumas officials from exercising jurisdiction in Roop County.[348] Pierce ignored the injunction and the next day arrested the Roop County sheriff, William Naileigh.[349] He dispatched his deputy, Byers, to arrest Judge Ward. Afterwards, Byers and Pierce were to meet at Lanigar's Ranch outside of Susanville.

Byers made the arrest and started for Lanigar's. Meanwhile, Isaac Roop, who had been an observer in the battle of injunctions, decided the Plumas County officials were going too far. He gathered 6 Roop County men, who armed themselves and started after Byers. Along the way, Roop met John Dow, who was walking along carrying an ax. He joined the group. Before Roop got to the ranch, he stopped the men and went ahead to talk to the Plumas officials.[350] Pierce had already started for Quincy with Naileigh in tow. Exactly what happened at

Lanigar's is not clear, but Roop came off second best in the debate or scuffle which occurred, and Byers, with Ward, started for Quincy.[351] Roop did not give up that easily. He gathered his men and started after Byers. The party overtook him after a speedy chase and Byers, seeing Dow with the ax, remarked that he could not defend himself against men armed with axes, and surrendered.[352] They all returned to Lanigar's. Roop allowed Byers to send a message to Pierce who was some miles toward Quincy. When Pierce heard of Byer's capture, he released Naileigh on parole and started in all haste to Quincy for reinforcements.[353]

Briefly, the events followed in this order: Naileigh, after his release, returned to Susanville and issued a call for the citizens of Roop County to arm and prepare for the Plumas County forces. The Roop officials formally arrested Byers for contempt of the Roop Court.[354] Since there was no jail, he was to board at Isaac Roop's home and report occasionally to Miss Susan Roop, Isaac's daughter, who had arrived from the east that January.[355] Because Byers was friendly with most of the citizens of the area, he wanted a peaceful settlement. He and the Roop officials arranged his release so he could return to Quincy and present the jurisdictional dispute before the District Court of California. After a decision, either side could appeal to the California Supreme Court whose decision would be accepted as final.[356] The Roop County forces also appealed to Nevada Territory for an opinion in the case. Isaac Roop, Isaac Baggs, H. W. Jennings, Ward, Naileigh and Parkington addressed a letter to Judge Mott on February 10, 1863, asking for advice.[357] Mott upheld the contentions of the Roop County advocates, but he did not deliver his decision until after the "war" had taken place.[358]

Although many of the citizens of Susanville and Plumas County preferred peaceful settlement, the participants were too involved to see any solution. On the evening of Friday, February 13, 1863, Sheriff Pierce returned with his posse of over 90 men and camped at Lanigar's Ranch.[359] He took a small group of men and entered Susanville, arresting Ward and Naileigh, but releasing them on parole again, if they promised to surrender when Pierce wanted them.[360] The Roop County men did not want to see their county officers taken away again, so a number of them gathered and formed a plan to further the defiance of the Plumas sheriff. They occupied Roop's original log cabin, which was now being used as a shed. Then they took into custody their own sheriff and judge, Naileigh and Ward, to prevent the Plumas authorities from coming to claim them.[361]

When Pierce and his Plumas force entered town the next morning, they found the Roop County forces in the cabin, soon to become known as Fort Defiance. The opposing forces conferred throughout the day, but the men in the fort would not yield the two officials, even though Ward and Naileigh were willing to surrender to avoid bloodshed.[362] At ten o'clock on Sunday morning, February 15, the shooting began. Pierce had ensconced about 40 of his Plumas forces in a feed stable 150 to 200 feet from Fort Defiance. To further secure the building, he had the flooring torn up and nailed on the side toward the fort. Six men were sent out to pull in some timbers which lay near the barn. The Roop County men let it be known that such action would bring gunfire. The Plumas men decided it was a bluff and went ahead. Some of the men in the fort opened fire, and one of the Plumas men outside the barn was hit in the thigh.[363] The log was pulled in and the man rescued. The Plumas group returned the fire.

For the rest of the morning and into the afternoon, the sporadic firing continued. Although Pierce thought there were from 75 to 100 men in the small Roop cabin,[364] only about 35 were there at any one time.[365] During the firing, two of the Plumas shots managed to hit men within the Roop cabin. One of these was Judge Ward, who received a serious wound in the collarbone.[366] Both of the wounded were taken to Roop's home where Susan Roop acted as a nurse.

During the firing, Isaac Roop had been in and out of his old cabin, now the Roop County fort. Nearly all of his efforts were directed towards mediating the struggle.[367] He and others talked with both sides. At two o'clock, Roop and the peacemakers were successful, and the opposing groups agreed to a truce of three hours.[368] When the time was up, the two forces had reached no agreement, so they extended the truce until nine o'clock the next morning. During the evening, Pierce received a petition signed by 65 residents of Susanville beseeching him to withdraw.[369] Actually, most of the residents of the town were not involved in the fight and were afraid that if the two contingents did not reach an agreement, the whole town would be involved.[370]

Pierce saw that he had no reinforcements due for some time and that the Roop forces were growing. In view of the demands of many citizens, he decided to withdraw his forces, providing the whole conflict was referred to the Governor of California and Governor of Nevada for peaceful settlement.[371] "Rough" Elliott, the leader of the Roop County forces in the cabin, agreed, and the "war" ended.

During the conciliation meeting at which the foregoing agreements were made, Isaac Roop and Daniel Murray, representing Roop County, and William J. Young and Israel Jones, representing Plumas County, were appointed to draw up a statement of the events which occurred and send it to the Governors.[372]

The activities of Isaac Roop were important in this "war." He was responsible for some of the anger which started the difficulty at Lanigar's Ranch. When the fighting became serious, however, he took no part and wished to avoid a serious incident. As the leader of the peacemakers during and after the fighting, he was chiefly responsible for avoiding serious loss of life. If the truce had not been permanent, another day's battle could have been disastrous. One writer states that the "Sagebrush War was saved from being a war; therein lies much of its importance."[373]

Governor Stanford received the report of the four-man commission. He appointed Judge Robert Robinson to represent California in the negotiation with Nevada.[374] Acting-Governor Orion Clemens of Nevada appointed John E. Lovejoy to represent Nevada.[375] The commission held various conferences and visited Susanville. The result was the ordering of a joint survey of the 120th meridian boundary in the summer of 1863.[376] The survey, completed by Kidder and Ives, showed that Honey Lake was well inside California.[377] California accepted the line on April 4, 1864,[378] and Nevada accepted it on February 7, 1865.[379]

Isaac Roop and the Roop County adherents had failed in their efforts for eastern slope unity. After years of fighting for Nevada citizenship, the immovable boundary line had placed them in California.

Fort Defiance, Roop's Log House at Honey Lake.
Courtesy of Brian Bauman

CHAPTER FIVE
THE CLOSING YEARS

The advocates of the defunct Roop County, Nevada, had, by force turned their backs upon the Great Basin. But this did not mean that they would embrace Plumas County as their own. Soon after the Honey Lakers found they were in California to stay, talk of the formation of a separate county began. Not all the advocates of the plan were disgruntled ex-Nevadans. Some of the legislators in Sacramento had expressed opinions that the establishment of a new county would end the difficulties between the Honey Lake Valley residents and the Plumas County officials.[380] Even the Plumas County Assemblyman, R. A. Clark, was in favor of such a measure. Therefore, in February, 1864, he introduced a bill to create Lassen County from the northeastern sections of Plumas and Shasta Counties.[381]

The naming of the proposed county caused a great deal of debate. James D. Byers, who, as Plumas County deputy sheriff, had been one of the principals in the Sagebrush War, became an advocate of the new county. Throughout the years he was a Plumas official, his residence had been near Janesville, just a few miles south of Susanville.[382] This was one of the reasons he had been conciliatory in the conflict and willing to cooperate with the Honey Lake Valley citizens in a just solution to their problem. During the legislative session at the end of 1863, he went to Sacramento to urge upon the Plumas officials the creation of the new county. Before he departed, many of the citizens considered the naming of the county if the mission were successful. One reliable source states that some of the leading men of the area, including Byers, agreed that the county, when formed, should be named Roop County, in honor of its leading citizen, and in memory of its predecessor, Roop County, Nevada.[383] The fact that Byers did not do this when he got to Sacramento may have been due to a grudge he held toward Roop for capturing him while he took Judge Ward toward Quincy in February, 1863.[384] It is difficult to determine whether there is any truth in this allegation. Whatever the case, after the publicity the "War" had brought to the name of Roop in the months just previous to the legislative meeting, it is doubtful that such a controversial name would have received the favor of the lawmakers, especially those from Plumas County, who necessarily were the first to consider the proposition. They looked more favorably upon the well-known and certainly less controversial name of the deceased pioneer, Peter Lassen.

The Plumas and Shasta delegations in Sacramento approved of the new county, and the bill went through the Legislature rapidly.[385] On April 1, 1864, Governor Low signed the bill into law, creating Lassen County.[386]

Isaac Roop temporarily retired from public life after the exciting events of the Sagebrush War. He could hardly expect to have a driving interest in the affairs of California government after having spent ten years trying to separate himself from it politically.

In 1862, Roop's daughter, Susan, had come from Ohio where she had been living with her grandparents.[387] For the first time since coming to California, Isaac Roop was able to enjoy a touch of family life. During the same year, he moved into a new residence on the main street in Susanville. He had sold some lots to a Harry Thompson. Thompson had built a house, but was unable to pay for the lots. Roop took them back, and he and Susan moved into the house. Roop improved the grounds and made the place into a beautiful residence. The people of Susanville considered it one of the finest homes in town.[388]

Isaac Roop was the first postmaster of Susanville.[389] He had been keeping an unofficial post office since 1859, but the mail deliveries were often uncertain. Finally in July, 1862, the federal government established two regular routes to Susanville. One came from Oroville and the other from Red Bluff.[390]

For Roop, the year just after the creation of Lassen County was a political lull. He held his postmaster's job and devoted his time to the building of the town. His days of pioneering in the area had passed. The town was well established, and now that the jurisdictional disputes were over, the average citizen led a busy but quiet life. For this reason, there is little record of Roop's activities from 1864 to 1869. The best source of material is the history of Lassen County written by Asa M. Fairfield, who was a pioneer himself. Most of the account of these years is based upon his work.

Since Isaac Roop was the first resident of the valley, he became a big land holder. In the days of Nataqua, however, he had given away much of his original claim in town lots, in order to encourage the growth of his town. In the ensuing years, Roop continued to deal in land. He sold lots to various settlers from the land in his original claim. In 1861, he sold the land upon which the Roop House stands to a Dr. Brown.[391] Thus, when the Sagebrush War two years later centered around Fort Defiance, the re-christened Roop House, Isaac no longer owned the building or the land.

Also in 1861, Roop sold his sawmill, a few miles west of town on the Susan River, to E. V. and L. D. Spencer.[392] He retained the water rights from Susan Creek, though, and leased the water company. During the next year, he sold a corner lot in Susanville to the Methodist Episcopal Church for one dollar.[393] The church officials never built upon the land, however. Roop also donated land for the site of the Court House in Susanville. On another occasion, he settled a large bill with the local general store of Hosselkus and Harvey by selling one of his town lots to them.[394]

The Civil War was raging during this period, and Susanville, like other loyal communities in California, wished to show its allegiance to the Union. The best way to accomplish this was to organize the Home Guard. Although the group became a part of the California National Guard in 1864, it was just a more formal version of the "Honey Lake Rangers" of the Nataqua days. Records show that Isaac Roop was a member of the organization throughout the Civil War. His highest rank was listed as Fourth Corporal.[395]

Isaac Roop ran for elective office for the first time in Lassen County on September 6, 1865. In an election in which 489 votes were cast, Roop became the District Attorney of Lassen County.[396] Roop had first qualified to practice law under the Nevada courts in 1862. At that time, he and the others in the class of candidates appearing before Judge Mott in Susanville had qualified in typical frontier style. Roop had been told beforehand that one of the questions Judge Mott would ask concerned the definition of a corporation. The proper answer was that a corporation was a creature of the law, having certain powers and duties of a natural person. When called upon for a definition, Roop is reputed to have answered "A corporation is a band of fellows without any soul, of who the law is a creature, who have some powers and take a great many more and entirely ignore the statutory duties imposed upon them." Judge Mott admitted the whole class.[397]

The chief excitement in Susanville during these years was over the Humboldt and Idaho mining booms.[398] Since Susanville was on the direct route from central California to either Idaho or northwestern Nevada, it prospered by the rush.[399] In April, 1863, John Bidwell, J. C. Mandeville and others of Chico obtained a franchise from the California Legislature to operate a toll road from Chico to Honey Lake Valley.[400] At the same time, Pierce and Francis, with the backing of Bidwell, ran a passenger and mail service from Chico to Idaho every week. The citizens of Susanville cooperated in improving the route to increase travel. In July, 1865, the first stage from Chico to Idaho passed through Susanville. Isaac Roop was the advisory agent for this line.[401] The route was not too successful because of the winter snows in the mountain passes and the need for additional work on the roads. The extension of the western link of the transcontinental railroad across the Sierra in 1868 killed the venture.

Roop was not very active as District Attorney. When his term expired in 1867, however, he did run successfully for re-election.[402] During the next year, however, Roop, either by choice or oversight, failed to file his bond or take the oath of office in the prescribed time, and so vacated the office.[403] The Lassen County Board of Supervisors appointed W. R. Harrison to fill the unexpired term on July 4, 1868.[404]

During 1867, Roop had one last visit from Old Winnemucca, the Chief of the Paiutes of Pyramid Lake. The chief came into Susanville accompanied by about ten warriors. They caused a great deal of excitement as they approached town, and some of the Indians turned back when they saw that some of the residents were beginning to arm themselves. Winnemucca and one brave came ahead and sought out Isaac Roop. The chief showed Roop letters from whites in Nevada telling of his peaceful intentions.[405] He had come asking about the possibility of hunting and fishing in the area of Eagle Lake, a few miles north of Susanville. The town had changed since the early days when the Indians came about frequently, and a crowd gathered around Roop and there was talk of taking Winnemucca prisoner. Roop would not stand for such action and told the crowd that he and Winnemucca had made a peace agreement years before, and that the Chief had helped him on many occasions. He said that they would have to take him before Winnemucca. Roop then received support from some of the other older settlers, including Weatherlow, Ward, Naileigh and Cutler Arnold.[406] This group took Winnemucca to Roop's home where he stayed a few days until some soldiers on their way north to Fort Bidwell took the Chief safely out of town.

This incident shows the confidence which Roop and Winnemucca had in each other. As related previously, Roop had talked with Winnemucca the first year he settled in the valley and, with Peter Lassen, he had made treaties which saved the settlement a great deal of trouble from the Paiutes. Roop helped the Indians whenever he had the opportunity. During the difficult winter of 1859-1860, he had found Indians in Truckee Meadows freezing as he journeyed to his inauguration as Provisional Governor of Nevada Territory. He had attempted to feed some of them, but they would not eat, fearing the food of the whites, who had invaded their country in great numbers that year.[407] In 1862, Winnemucca came to a ranch near Lassen Creek in the lower end of Honey Lake Valley, and asked for food and ammunition with which to kill game. The ranchers went to Susanville, and with the help of Roop, filled a wagon with blankets and ammunition to give to the Indians. Winnemucca and his braves took their gifts and went away, harming no one.[408]

When Roop was a Nevada legislator in 1861, his interest in the Indians' welfare caused him to favor the sale of arms and ammunition to them when no hostilities existed between the two races. Roop felt that, since the influx of the white men in the Comstock mining boom, the Indian could no longer support himself on the bow and arrow. He also said that if the bill under consideration (to prohibit all arming of Indians) should pass without his recommended exceptions, he would "give the Indians in his neighborhood guns and ammunition and pay the fine for it if enforced until his last dollar was gone."[409] If more of the pioneers of the westward advance had felt as Roop did, there may have been a much saner approach to the conflict which was bound to arise.

After Roop vacated the District Attorney's office, he did little which is known today. By this time, 14 years after he had built the first cabin in Honey Lake Valley, he held the position in Susanville of a "senior citizen," though he was only 46 years of age. Now that stability had come to his settlement, Roop probably looked forward to reaping the fruits of his years of effort for its well being. But this was not to be. During the second week in February, 1869, he became seriously ill.[410] He died on February 14, 1869. The Susanville paper contained this obituary:

> Governor Roop was a man of enlarged mind and noble charities, true in his friendships, kind in his disposition, and manly in his character. If human weakness were his, they were of the heart. If to poor human nature it is given to err, his errors were the promptings of a generous soul unmixed with meanness and unclouded by the darker shades of malevolent passions. The genial

> smile, and the hand of hospitality ever ready to be
> extended, will be missed by the stranger when he visits
> the town of Susanville. The death of Governor Roop
> will create a vacuum difficult to be filled. The
> community in which he lived so long could better have
> lost other men than him.[411]

Isaac Roop was an American pioneer. One could consider him typical of the class of men who worked their way to prominence on the frontier by their leadership of the mass of men who moved across the continent. Determined out-of-doorsmen, adaptable and usually self-educated, the type was not content to follow in ordinary paths.

One cannot, however, fit an individual into a stereotype. Each person has his own complex of motive and drives which direct the course of his actions. In these characteristics, Roop was no different than anyone else. But Isaac Roop was a leader. He made decisions and then followed through. With leadership he combined his greatest asset -- sincere and true friendship for others. He greeted every immigrant who came past his cabin in the early Honey Lake Valley days, and he was always ready to help the friend or stranger who needed aid. Sometimes his friendliness led to impracticality. He never became wealthy, although he had the opportunity. He gave away much of this land and put money into the development of his town. This may also have been a manifestation of a slight strain of Utopian dreaming about the future of Honey Lake Valley and Susanville. Isaac Roop was not a visionary, though. Neither was he a rebel, despite his involvement in the various extra-legal political ventures of the eastern slope. Throughout his Honey Lake career, his first interest was the settlement. He saw that it needed an adequate government, and he set out to achieve it. As with any challenge, he met it with vigor. When he saw that his goal, political unity of the western Great Basin, was unattainable, he shifted his aim and adapted to the inevitable.

Isaac Roop's background and character suited him for more than local interests in his later life. If he had lived past the age of 47, northeastern California might have had a significant spokesmen in state and national affairs. As it happened, Isaac Roop had already accomplished enough to give him a deserved, but limited, recognition. It is time that this recognition spread.

ENDNOTES

[1] A. T. Bruce, "Isaac N. Roop," in Oscar T. Shuck, Representative and Leading Men of the Pacific, (San Francisco, 1870), p. 405.

[2] Illustrated History of Plumas, Lassen, and Sierra Counties, Fariss and Smith, pub., (San Francisco, 1882), p. 412. Herein-after cited as Illustrated History.

[3] Isaac Roop, [Book of Memoranda and Clippings], MS in the possession of Isaac Roop's grandson, Mr. Medford R. Arnold of Susanville, California. In it, Isaac Roop records his ancestry as follows: "David Roop moved from the Highlands of Germany in 1693 to New York City. He begat William Roop who was born 1709 New York City. He begat John Roop who was born in 1740 Pa He begat Joseph Roop who was born in 1765 Pa He begat Joseph Roop who was born in 1790 MD He begat Isaac Roop who was born in 1822 MD."

[4] Information obtained in correspondence with Mr. Wendell Roop of Sewall, New Jersey. Mr. Roop believes that he and Isaac Roop have common ancestry in Germany. He has carried out diligent research of the Roop family throughout the United States and has furnished this writer with Isaac Roop Goes West, (n.p., 1958). 10pp.

[5] Loc. cit.

[6] Loc. cit.

[7] J. M. Guinn, History of the State of California and Biographical Record of the Sierras, (Chicago, 1906), p. 335.

[8] Bruce, loc. cit.

[9] Illustrated History, loc. cit.

[10] Bruce, loc cit.

[11] Wendell Roop, loc cit.

[12] Loc. cit.

[13] Asa Merrill Fairfield, Fairfield's Pioneer History of Lassen County, California, (San Francisco, [1916]), p. 481.

[14]   Illustrated History, loc, cit.

[15]   Guinn, loc cit.

[16]   Bruce, loc cit.

[17]   Loc. cit.

[18]   Illustrated History, loc. cit.

[19]   Wendell Roop, loc. cit.; Bruce, loc. cit.

[20]   Bruce, loc cit. Of Isaac's children, Susan came to California in 1862, Isaiah, a member of the 23rd Ohio Infantry died during the Civil War, and John, in the 7th Iowa Infantry during the War, became a doctor and settled in Oklahoma. Fairfield, op. cit., p. 481.

[21]   Georgia Willis Read and Ruth Gaines, ed., Gold Rush, The Journals, Drawings and Other Papers of J. Goldsborough Bruff, (Columbia University Press, 1944), Vol. II, p. 926.

[22]   Joseph Roop, Josiah Roop's Business Records at Shasta, California, MS in the California Historical Society Library, San Francisco. Shasta is six miles west of present-day Redding.

[23]   Fairfield, op. cit., p. 482.

[24]   Hubert Howe Bancroft, History of California, Vol. IV, (San Francisco, 1882), p. 347.

[25]   Fairfield, loc. cit.

[26]   Hubert Howe Bancroft, History of California, Vol. VI, (San Francisco, 1888), p. 492.

[27]   "Journal of Pierson Barton Reading...", Phillip Beakert, ed., Quarterly of Society of California Pioneer, VII, (1930), pp. 148-198. See also the "Notes on the Journal of P. B. Reading," Ibid., IX, (1932), p. 67.

[28]   Bancroft, op. cit., Vol. VI, p. 17, 492, map p. 5; "A Brief Biography of P. B. Reading," Quarterly of the Society of California Pioneers, VII, (1930), pp. 139-141.

29 Bancroft, op. cit., Vol. VI, p. 69. Bancroft quotes Sutter's diary, stating Sutter, Reading and Edwin Kemble left Sutter's fort on April 18 and were gone four days.

30 Rosena A. Giles, Shasta County, California, A History, (Oakland, 1949), p. 187, 188; Bancroft, op. cit., p. 493; Charles A. Shurtleff, "Shasta," Quarterly of the Society of California Pioneers, VII (1930), p. 103.

31 Giles, op. cit., p. 188; Shurtleff, op. cit., p. 107.

32 Giles, op. cit., p. 107.

33 Shurtleff, op. cit., p. 105; Possibly the change was made to avoid confusing Reading's Bar on the Trinity with Reading's Diggings or Redding's Diggings, which seems to have been applied to both this town and the whole area. Bancroft, op. cit., Vol. VI, p. 492, calls the town Reading's Upper Spring. For a discussion, see Red and Gaines, ed., op. cit., Vol, II, n. 43, p. 1055.

34 Giles, op. cit., p. 72.

35 Illustrated History, op. cit., p. 412; Bruce, op. cit., p. 406.

36 Shasta Courier as quoted in the Alta California (San Francisco), August 20, 1851.

37 Illustrated History, op. cit., p. 406.

38 Shasta Courier, March 12, 1852, as quoted in the Sacramento Union, March 20, 1852, p. 1.

39 Giles, op. cit., p. 51.

40 Walter N. Frickstad, A Century of California Post Offices, 1848 to 1954, (Oakland, 1955), p. 280. The author quotes official post-office records in the National Archives.

41 Shasta Courier, August 7, 1852, p. 2, 3. A rare issue in the California Section, State Library, Sacramento.

42 Statutes of California, 1850, p. 58-63; Owen C. Coy, California County Boundaries, (Berkeley, 1923), p. 69.

43 Myrtle McNamar, Way Back When, (Cottonwood, California, 1954), p. 54.

[44]   Sacramento Union, January 13, 1852, p. 1.

[45]   Shasta Courier, April 16, 1853, supplement.

[46]   Josiah Roop, op. cit.

[47]   Loc. cit. Isaac Roop's name does appear in transactions involving considerable sums.

[48]   Shasta Courier, August 7, 1852, p. 2.

[49]   Sacramento Union. May 11, 1852, p. 2.

[50]   Shasta Courier, August 7, 1852, p. 3.

[51]   Loc. cit.

[52]   Loc. cit.

[53]   McNamar, op. cit., p. 37.

[54]   Giles, op. cit., p. 63.

[55]   Alta California, June 7, 1852, p. 1.

[56]   Shasta Courier, April 23, 1853, p. 2.

[57]   They were not the first through the area. In October, 1850, Peter Lassen and J. G. Bruff, hunting for the mythical Gold Lake of the Sierras, had camped in Honey Lake Valley. Lassen had named the lake on an earlier trip that year. See Read and Gaines, op. cit., Vol. II, pp. 866, 868, sketches facing 866, 868, pp. 907, 925, 1088, 1090.

[58]   Asa Merrill Fairfield, Fairfield's Pioneer History of Lassen County, California, (San Francisco, [1916]), p. 17.

[59]   Shasta Courier, September 17, 1853, p. 1, reprints the original description of the trip and route from the June 19, 1852 issue.

[60]   Shasta Courier, June, 1852, as quoted in Fairfield, op. cit., p. 18.

[61]   "A Jaunt to Honey Lake Valley and Nobles' Pass," <u>Hutchings' Illustrated California Magazine</u>, Vol. I, June, 1857, pp. 537-539; <u>Shasta Courier</u>, August 7, 1852, p. 2, November 19, 1853, p. 1.

[62]   Leon O. Whitsell, <u>One Hundred Years of Masonry in California</u>, (San Francisco, 1950), pp. 65, 411, 1413, 1426-1428.

[63]   Isaac Roop, <u>op. cit.</u>

[64]   <u>Shasta Courier</u>, November 27, 1852, as quoted in Giles, <u>op. cit.</u>, p. 110.

[65]   Wendell Roop, <u>op. cit.</u>

[66]   <u>Shasta Courier</u>, March 12, 1853; March 19, 1853.

[67]   <u>Ibid.</u>, April 2, 1853; April 23, 1853.

[68]   Bancroft, <u>op. cit.</u>, Vol. VI, p. 655.

[69]   <u>Shasta Courier</u>, June 18, 1853, p. 1.

[70]   <u>Loc. cit.</u>

[71]   Giles, <u>op. cit.</u>, p. 105.

[72]   <u>Shasta Courier</u>, <u>loc. cit.</u>

[73]   <u>Loc. cit.</u>; also June 25, 1853, p. 1.

[74]   Asa Merrill Fairfield, <u>Fairfield's Pioneer History of Lassen County, California</u>, (San Francisco, [1916]), p. 21; <u>Illustrated History of Plumas, Lassen, and Sierra Counties</u>, Fariss and Smith, pub., (San Francisco, 1882), p. 341, hereafter cited as <u>Illustrated History</u>.

[75]   <u>Roop's Record Book</u>, MS, p. 1, as reproduced in William N. Davis, Jr., <u>California East of the Sierra</u>, (Ph.D. Thesis, unpub., University of California, 1942), p. 122. Page 24 of this work is a copy of Dr. Davis' reproduction. See also fn. #44, p. 38.

[76]   Davis, <u>op. cit.</u>, p. 120-121.

[77]   Almost all of the earliest extant issues of the Shasta Courier contain some information about the route or recent immigration over it.

[78]   Shasta Courier, August 7, 1852, p. 3. A rare issue in the California Section, State Library, Sacramento.

[79]   Ibid., p. 2.

[80]   Israel C. Russell, Geological History of Lake Lahontan, A Quaternary Lake of Northwestern Nevada, U. S. Geological Survey Monographs, Vol XI, (Washington, 1885), pp. 1, 2, 11, 12, 32.

[81]   Ibid., p. 32.

[82]   Ibid., p. 31.

[83]   Ibid., p. 12, 18.

[84]   George and Bliss Hinkle, Sierra-Nevada Lakes, (New York, 1949). American Lake Series, Milo Quaife, gen. ed.

[85]   Davis, op. cit., p. 6.

[86]   Hinkle, loc. cit.

[87]   Fairfield, op. cit., p. 23.

[88]   Shasta Courier, December 3, 1853, p. 2; April 1, 1854,p. 2.

[89]   Illustrated History, op. cit., p. 341.

[90]   Loc. cit.

[91]   E. G. Beckwith, Report of Exploration for a Route for the Pacific Railroad, on the Line of the Forty-first Parallel of North Latitude, 1854, 33d Cong., 2d Sess., Senate Exec. Doc., the valley, the Susan River, Honey Lake and Roop's house are found on pp. 48, 49, 65, 69, 70, 93.

[92]   Roop's Record Book, op. cit., in Davis, op. cit., p. 122.

[93]   Roop's log house (illustration, p. 73), still stands in downtown Susanville as a solid reminder of these early days.

[94]   Hinkle, op. cit., p. 115. The Roop House Register, MS is in the California Section, State Library, Sacramento.

[95]   Fairfield, op. cit., p. 22-23.

[96]   Figures and dates in this paragraph are from the Roop House Register, op. cit.

[97]   Roop's Record Book, op. cit., as reproduced from Davis on p. 25.

[98]   Fairfield, op. cit., pp. 25, 473.

[99]   Roop House Register, op. cit. Entry of August 25, 1854.

[100] Shasta Courier, October 21, 1854, p. 2.

[101] Illustrated History, op. cit., p. 341; Fairfield, op. cit., p. 25.

[102] Illustrated History, op. cit., p. 341.

[103] Fairfield, op. cit., p. 25.

[104] Page 2.

[105] Shasta Courier, December 8, 1854, p. 2.

[106] "Memorial of the Citizens of Shasta, January 28, 1855." MS, filed under Petitions to the Legislature, 1855, California State Archives, Sacramento.

[107] Illustrated History, op. cit., p. 342.

[108] Loc. cit.

[109] Roop Record Book, quoted in Fairfield, op. cit., p. 28.

[110] Roop House Register, op. cit.

[111] Fairfield, op. cit., p. 28.

[112] Ibid., p. 28, 30.

[113] Illustrated History, op. cit., p. 343.

[114] Roop House Register, op. cit.

[115] Ibid.

[116] Discussed on pp. 27-29.

[117] Roop's Record Book also contained copies of Roop's original claim of 1853 and other claims made prior to May 1, 1856. The book, used extensively by Fairfield at the turn of this century, was in the Lassen County Clerk's Office, Susanville, in 1942, when Dr. Davis consulted it and had the first page reproduced. Recent inquiry and search by Mr. Wendell Roop and this writer has failed to uncover it.

[118] Roop's Record Book, as quoted in Fairfield, op. cit., p. 31.

[119] Fairfield, op. cit. p. 31. Fairfield actually located most of the claims at the time he wrote his history of Lassen County. The claims are listed in 31ff., 55ff., 97ff., 149ff., 188ff., 240ff., 257ff., 261.

[120] Ibid., p. 32-34.

[121] Davis, op. cit., p. 127.

[122] Fairfield, op. cit., p. 40.

[123] Statutes of California, 1850, p. 24, Article XII; U. S. Statutes at Large, (1851), p. 452.

[124] J. Ross Browne, Report of the Debates in the Convention of California on the Formation of the State Constitution in September and October, 1949, (Washington, D. C., 1850).

[125] Roop House Register, op. cit.

[126] Illustrated History, op. cit., p. 344.

[127] Loc. cit. Roop kept a valuable record of all the meetings held by the settlers under the laws of Nataqua Territory. This book, not to be confused with Roop's Record Book, a list of filings, is quoted extensively in Illustrated History. It disappeared at the turn of the century.

[128] Davis, op. cit., p. 159.

[129]   Illustrated History, op. cit.; Swartzlow, op. cit.

[130]   Davis, op. cit., Chapter VIII, pp. 157-184.

[131]   Ibid., p. 162.

[132]   Illustrated History, op. cit., pp. 344-346.

[133]   Ibid., p. 345.

[134]   Loc. cit.

[135]   Charles H. Shinn, Mining Camps. A Study in American Frontier Government, (New York, 1885), pp. 232-258.

[136]   Davis, op. cit., p. 163.

[137]   Fairfield, op. cit., p. 261.

[138]   Ibid., p. 35.

[139]   Illustrated History, op. cit., pp. 348, 349.

[140]   Loc. cit.

[141]   Davis, op. cit., p. 167.

[142]   Fairfield, op. cit., pp. 39-40.

[143]   Roop House Register, op. cit.

[144]   Fairfield, op. cit., pp. 63, 94.

[145]   Roop House Register, op. cit.

[146]   Illustrated History, op. cit., p. 394.

[147]   Fairfield, op. cit., p. 63.

[148]   Roop House Register, op. cit.

[149] Isaac Roop, "Honey Lake Correspondence," in Shasta Courier, May 8, 1858, p. 1.; Illustrated History, op cit., p. 412.

[150] Illustrated History, op. cit., p. 394.

[151] Fairfield, op.cit., p. 187.

[152] [Myron Angel] ed., History of Nevada, Thompson and West pub., (Oakland, 1881), p. 31-32; Hubert Howe Bancroft, History of Nevada, Colorado and Wyoming, (San Francisco, 1890), p. 69.

[153] Angel, op. cit., p. 32.

[154] Statutes of California, (1852), p. 193.

[155] California Senate Journal, (1853), p. 90.

[156] Ibid., 4th Sess. Appendix, p. 46.

[157] Angel, op. cit., p. 33.

[158] Utah (Terr.) Statutes, (1855), p. 258, 398.

[159] Angel, op. cit., p. 38; Bancroft, op. cit., p. 76.

[160] Bancroft, op. cit., p. 76-77.

[161] Sherman Day, "Report of a Survey of a Portion of the Eastern Boundary of California and of a Reconnaissance of the Old Carson-Johnson Immigrant Road over the Sierra Nevada." (Sacramento, 1855), pp. 81-96. California Pamphlets, Vol. 26, Bancroft Library.

[162] California Assembly Journal, (1856), p. 141.

[163] State Miscellaneous Documents, 34th Congress, 1st Sess., p. 48.

[164] For a complete study of the boundary question, see Beulah Hershiser, "The Adjustment of the Boundaries of Nevada," First Biennial Report of the Nevada Historical Society, 1907-1908, (Carson City, 1909), pp. 121-134; and William N. Davis, Jr., California East of the Sierra, (unpub., Ph. D. thesis, 1942), pp. 97-118.

[165] Effie M. Mack, <u>Nevada: A History of the State from the Earliest Times through the Civil War</u>, (Glendale, Calif., 1936), pp. 143-173.

[166] Angel, <u>op. cit.</u>, p. 42.

[167] Bancroft, <u>op. cit.</u>, p. 82.

[168] Angel, <u>op. cit.</u>, p. 42.

[169] <u>Ibid.</u>, p. 43.

[170] Davis, <u>op. cit.</u>, p. 179.

[171] The convention was reported in the San Francisco <u>Daily Evening Bulletin</u>, October 6-20, 1857.

[172] Angel, <u>op. cit.</u>, p. 42.

[173] San Francisco <u>Daily Evening Bulletin</u>, July 17, 1861, p. 1.

[174] Angel, <u>op. cit.</u>, pp. 42-45.

[175] Angel, <u>op. cit.</u>, pp. 42-45, quotes the memorial <u>in extenso</u>.

[176] <u>Loc. cit.</u>

[177] <u>Loc. cit.</u>

[178] <u>Loc. cit.</u>

[179] Davis, <u>op. cit.</u>, p. 168.

[180] <u>Illustrated History of Plumas, Lassen, and Sierra Counties</u>, Fariss and Smith, pub., (San Francisco, 1882), pp. 350-352, hereinafter cited as <u>Illustrated History</u>.

[181] <u>Ibid.</u>, p. 351.

[182] <u>Loc. cit.</u>

[183] <u>Loc. cit.</u>

[184] <u>Ibid.</u>, p. 352.

[185] Ibid., p. 350.

[186] Quoted in Asa Merrill Fairfield, Fairfield's Pioneer History of Lassen County, California, (San Francisco, [1916]), pp. 80-81.

[187] This meeting was widely reported in the California press: Sacramento Daily Union, October 19, 1857, p. 1; San Francisco Alta California, October 21, 1857; San Francisco Daily Evening Bulletin, October 20, 21, 1857; Shasta Courier, October 17, 1857, p. 1.

[188] Shasta Courier, October 17, 1857, p. 1.

[189] Loc. cit.

[190] Loc. cit.

[191] Loc. cit.

[192] San Francisco Daily Evening Bulletin, October 20, 1857,   p. 3.

[193] Statutes of California, 1858, p. 350.

[194] Hershisher, op. cit., p. 124.

[195] Angel, op. cit., p. 46.

[196] Loc. cit.

[197] San Francisco Daily Evening Bulletin, April 9, 1858, p. 2.

[198] House Journal, 35th Cong., 1st Sess., pp. 789, 1221.

[199] Congressional Globe, 35th Gong., 1st Sess., p. 2122.

[200] San Francisco Daily Evening Bulletin, July 17, 1861, p. 1.

[201] Illustrated History, op. cit., pp. 354, 355.

[202] Bancroft, op. cit., pp. 84, 88-89.

[203] Angel, op. cit., p. 49.

[204] Loc. cit.

[205] Ibid., p. 62.

[206] Loc. cit.

[207] The primary source for the convention is the complete minutes in the Genoa Territorial Enterprise of July 30, 1859, which is reproduced in Angel, op. cit., pp. 69-72.

[208] The convention is also reported in the Alta California, July 27, August 10, 13, 20, 1859.

[209] Angel, Loc. cit.

[210] Loc. cit.

[211] Loc. cit.

[212] Loc. cit.

[213] Bancroft, op. cit., pp. 87-88.

[214] Angel, op. cit., p. 64.

[215] Placerville Semi-Weekly Observer quoted in Angel, op. cit., p. 63.

[216] Fairfield, op. cit., p. 162.

[217] Loc. cit.

[218] Angel, op. cit., p. 65. Why Mr. Preston felt that he had the authority to swear in an official of a territory not recognized by the federal government is unknown.

[219] Bancroft, op. cit., pp. 102-108; Angel, op. cit., pp. 51-61; Mack, op. cit., pp. 206-209.

[220] Carson City Territorial Enterprise, December 24, 1859, as quoted by Angel, op. cit., pp. 65-66.

[221] Loc. cit.; Alta California, September 28, 1859.

[222]   Angel, op. cit., p. 65.

[223]   Loc. cit.

[224]   Ibid., p. 66.

[225]   Fairfield, op. cit., p. 22-23.

[226]   A. L. Kroeber, Handbook of the Indians of California, Smithsonian Institution, Bureau of American Ethnology, Bulletin 78, (Washington, 1925), pp. 391, 569-570, 584, map in back of book.

[227]   Illustrated History, op. cit., p. 378.

[228]   Fairfield, op. cit., p. 82.

[229]   Loc. cit.

[230]   Shasta Courier, March 26, 1853, p. 2.

[231]   William Weatherlow, "Statement of William Weatherlow" MS (a handwritten copy, n. d.) in Fairfield Papers, California Section, State Library, Sacramento.

[232]   Fairfield, op. cit., p. 84.

[233]   Ibid., p. 86-87.

[234]   Loc. cit.; also San Francisco Daily Evening Bulletin, December 5, 1857, p. 1.

[235]   Sacramento Daily Union, October 27, 1857; San Francisco Daily Evening Bulletin, October 21, 1857, p. 2.; October 27, 1857; December 5, 1857, p. 1.

[236]   Ruby Johnson Swartzlow, Peter Lassen, Northern California's Trail-Blazer, (San Francisco, 1940), California Historical Society Reprint, p. 10.

[237]   Fairfield, op. cit., p.107-108, quotes the treaty in full.

[238]   Loc. cit.

[239]   Isaac Roop, "Honey Lake Correspondence." in Shasta Republican, May 8, 1858, p. 1. One of a series of signed letters from Roop to this paper.

[240] Loc. cit.

[241] Loc. cit.

[242] Isaac Roop, op. cit., May 22, 1858, p. 2; June 12, 1858, p. 1; Fairfield, op. cit., pp. 113-120.

[243] Swartzlow, op. cit., p. 10.

[244] Ibid., pp. 16-18; Fairfield, op. cit., pp. 171-178; Bancroft, op. cit., pp. 103-104.

[245] Fairfield, loc. cit.

[246] Sacramento Union, November 10, 1859, p. 2.

[247] Illustrated History, op. cit., pp. 379-380; Fairfield, op. cit., pp. 197-201.

[248] Fairfield, loc. cit.; Angel, op. cit., p. 148.

[249] Loc. cit.

[250] Quoted in Fairfield, op. cit., pp. 205-206; and Angel, op. cit., p. 149.

[251] Loc. cit.

[252] Bancroft, op. cit., pp. 208-216; Angel, op. cit., pp. 149-165.

[253] Fairfield, op. cit., pp. 222-225.

[254] Ibid., pp. 227-231.

[255] U. S. Statutes at Large, (1861), p. 210.

[256] Loc. cit.

[257] San Francisco Daily Evening Bulletin, July 22, 1861, p. 1.

[258] Hubert Howe Bancroft, History of Nevada, Colorado, and Wyoming, (San Francisco, 1890), p. 158.

[259] "Proclamations of Governor Nye," Executive Record [of Nevada Territory], 1861-1864, reproduced in U. S. Library of Congress, Records of the States of the U.

S., (Nevada, microfilm, D. 2, Reel 1a, Unit 5), University of Nevada Library, Reno. Original in the office of Secretary of State of Nevada, Carson City.

[260]   Loc. cit.

[261]   Bancroft, loc. cit.

[262]   Executive Record, op. cit., pp. 43-47.

[263]   Ibid., p. 46.

[264]   Bancroft, loc. cit.

[265]   [Myron Angel, ed.], History of Nevada, (Oakland, 1881), pp. 78, 79.

[266]   Executive Record, op. cit., p. 62.

[267]   Effie Mona Mack, Mark Twain in Nevada, (New York, 1947), p. 83-86. Orion Clemens had received his position as a reward for stumping Missouri for the election of Lincoln. His brother, Samuel Clemens or Mark Twain, accompanied him to Nevada and hoped to be appointed to the position of Assistant Secretary.

[268]   Mark Twain, Roughing It, (Hartford, 1877 ed.), p. 185-192.

[269]   Sacramento Union, October 7, 1861, p. 1.

[270]   Effie Mona Mack, Nevada: A History of the State from the Earliest Times through the Civil War, (Glendale, Calif., 1936),   p. 231.

[271]   Governor Nye's message is printed in full in the Sacramento Union, October 3, 1861, p. 1. The Union sent a reporter to Carson City and reported a detailed and accurate account of the entire proceedings.

[272]   Journal of the Council of the First Legislative Assembly of the Territory of Nevada , 1861, (San Francisco, 1862). Hereinafter cited as Council Journal, 1861.

[273]   Ibid., p. 42.

[274]   Sacramento Union, October 10, 1861, p. 1.; San Francisco Alta California, October 24, 1861, p. 1.

[275]   Council Journal, 1861, op. cit., pp. 42, 43.

[276] Ibid., p. 62.

[277] One of the sections of the laws passed in the revised Nataqua government of 1858 had read: "Owners of hogs shall be held to pay all damages their hogs may do between the first day of April and the first day of November." Illustrated History of Plumas, Lassen and Sierra Counties, Fariss and Smith, pub., (San Francisco, 1882), p. 354.

[278] Council Journal 1861, op. cit., p. 79-80.

[279] Sacramento Union, November 23, 1861, p. 1.

[280] Loc. cit.

[281] Laws of the Territory of Nevada, 1861, (San Francisco, 1862), p. 93, 94. Hereinafter cited as Nevada Laws, 1861.

[282] Council Journal, 1861, op. cit, p. 77, 114, 117-118.

[283] Mark Twain, op. cit., p. 192.

[284] Angel, op. cit., p. 80.

[285] Council Journal, 1861, op. cit., pp. 112, 163, 171.

[286] Sacramento Union, October 3, 1861, p. 1; Mack, Mark Twain, op. cit., p. 104.

[287] Council Journal, 1861, op. cit., p. 104.

[288] Mack, Mark Twain, op. cit., p. 104.

[289] Council Journal, 1861, op. cit., p. 94

[290] Nevada Laws, 1861, p. 32, 33.

[291] Sacramento Union, November 30, 1861, p. 4.

[292] Council Journal, 1861, op. cit., p. 258.

[293] Sacramento Union, October 25, 1861, p. 1, 2.

[294] Ibid., October 25, 28, November 4, 1861.

[295] Council Journal, 1861, op. cit., p. 113, 140.

[296] Ibid., p. 215.

[297] Sacramento Union, December 2, 1861, p. 8.

[298] Nevada Laws, 1861, p. 513; Council Journal, 1861, op. cit., p. 215.

[299] Sacramento Union, December 4, 1861, p. 1.

[300] Mark Twain, Roughing It, op. cit., pp. 241-247.

[301] Samuel L. Clemens, Mark Twain's Autobiography, Vol. II, (New York, 1924), p. 305.

[302] Bancroft, op. cit., p. 162.

[303] Sacramento Union, January 13, 23, 1862.

[304] San Francisco Alta California, March 19, 1862, p. 1, prints the memorial in extenso.

[305] Council Journal, 1861, op. cit., p. 85.

[306] Sacramento Union, October 25, 1861, p. 1.

[307] California Assembly Journal, 13th sess., (1862), p. 390; California Senate Journal, 13th sess., (1862), p. 387, 389.

[308] Alta California, March 22, 1862, p. 2.

[309] Loc. cit.; Sacramento Union, March 24, 1862, p. 3. Both give extensive coverage of the meeting and speeches.

[310] Loc. cit.

[311] Alta California, March 25, 1862, p. 2.

[312] "Second Annual Message of the Governor of Nevada Territory to the Legislature thereof, delivered November 13, 1862," Executive Record, 1861-1884, op. cit., p. 620.

[313] Loc. cit.

[314] California Senate Journal, 13th sess., (1862), p. 413, 485.

[315] Executive Record, 1861-1864, op. cit.

[316] California Senate Journal, 13th sess., (1862), p. 525-526; Beulah Hershisher, "The Adjustment of the Boundaries of Nevada," in Nevada Historical Society, First Biennial Report 1907-1908, (Carson City, 1909), p. 130.

[317] William N. Davis, Jr., California East of the Sierra, (Ph. D. thesis, University of California, unpub., 1942), p. 168.

[318] Statutes of California, (1857), p. 377.

[319] San Francisco Daily Evening Bulletin, October 20, 1857, p. 3.

[320] Statutes of California, (1858), p. 356-357; (1859), p. 313-314, 483-485; (1860), p. 409.

[321] Ibid., (1860), p. 184-185.

[322] U. S. Statutes at Large, (1860), p. 22.

[323] Statutes of California, (1861), p. 73-74, pp. 682-683.

[324] Hershisher, op. cit., p. 128.

[325] Ibid., p. 129; Davis, op. cit., p. 113.

[326] Davis, loc. cit.

[327] Asa Merrill Fairfield, Fairfield's Pioneer History of Lassen County, California, (San Francisco, 1916), pp. 77, 196.

[328] Ibid., p. 196.

[329] Ibid., p. 77; Davis, op. cit., p. 189.

[330] Davis, op. cit., p. 190-191.

[331] Loc. cit.

[332] Hershisher, op. cit., p. 130.

[333] Nevada Laws, 1861, pp. 50-52.

[334] Ibid., p. 52.

[335] Council Journal, 1861, op. cit., p. 215.

[336] Nevada Laws, 1861, p. 291; Sacramento Union, December 4, 1861, p. 1.

[337] Bancroft, op. cit., p. 162.

[338] Ibid., p. 164.

[339] Loc. cit.

[340] Fairfield, op. cit., p. 267; Davis, op. cit., p. 195.

[341] Angel, op. cit., p. 563. Unfortunately, the journals of this session of the Legislature were not printed so there is no complete record of the debate.

[342] Angel, loc. cit.

[343] Angel, loc. cit.

[344] Nevada Laws, 1862, p. 39.

[345] Illustrated History, op. cit., pp. 358-362; Fairfield, op. cit., pp. 311-321; Davis, op. cit., pp. 197-212; Harry L. Wells, "The Sagebrush Rebellion," Overland Monthly, n. s. XIII (March, 1889), pp. 253-259; Harry P. Bagley, "Trouble on the Nevada Border," Sacramento Bee, November 4, 1939, magazine section, p. 3. The account by Davis is the most complete and accurate.

[346] E. H. Pierce, "Report of Sheriff of Plumas County," (March 2, 1863), MS in Correspondence on the Boundary Question, California State Archives, Sacramento; also in Message of the Governor to the Legislature of California, no. 34, in Appendix to Journals of Senate and Assembly, pp. 4-6.

[347] Israel Jones, Dan Murray, Isaac Roop, Wm. J. Young, "Report of a Joint Committee at Susanville," (February 16, 1863) MS in Correspondence on the Boundary Question, California State Archives, Sacramento; also in Message of the Governor to the Legislature, op. cit., p. 7-8.

[348]   Davis, op. cit., p. 200.

[349]   E. H. Pierce, op. cit., p. 5.

[350]   Fairfield, op. cit., p. 313.

[351]   Loc. cit.; Davis, op. cit., p. 201.

[352]   Fairfield, loc. cit.

[353]   E. H. Pierce, op. cit., p. 5.

[354]   Davis, op. cit., p. 202.

[355]   Fairfield, loc. cit.

[356]   Davis, loc. cit.

[357]   Virginia City Territorial Enterprise, February 17, 1863, as quoted in San Francisco Daily Evening Bulletin, February 23, 1863, p. 1.

[358]   Ibid., February 20, 1863, in Orion Clemens, [Scrapbook 1861-1864]. Microfilm in the Bancroft Library, University of California.

[359]   E. H. Pierce, op. cit., p. 5.

[360]   Fairfield, op. cit., p. 314.

[361]   Israel Jones, Dan Murray, Isaac Roop, Wm. J. Young, op. cit., p. 7.

[362]   Fairfield, op. cit., p. 315.

[363]   Ibid., p. 317-318; Davis, op. cit., pp. 205-206.

[364]   E. H. Pierce, op. cit., p. 5.

[365]   Fairfield, op. cit., pp. 316-317.

[366]   Ibid., p. 319.

[367]   Ibid., pp. 319-320.

[368]   Israel Jones, et al. op. cit., p. 7.

[369]   E. H. Pierce, op. cit., p. 320.

[370]   Fairfield, op. cit., p. 320.

[371]   Illustrated History, op. cit., p. 361.

[372]   Angel, op. cit., pp. 100-101.

[373]   Davis, op. cit., p. 209.

[374]   "Letter of Governor Stanford to Judge Robinson," (March 4, 1863), Message of the Governor to the Legislature of California, op. cit., p. 8.

[375]   Angel, op. cit., p. 101.

[376]   Statutes of California, (1863), pp. 617-718; Nevada Laws, (1863), pp. 139, 864.

[377]   Fairfield, op. cit., p. 328.

[378]   Statutes of California, (1864), pp. 506-507.

[379]   Angel, op. cit., p. 102.

[380]   William N. Davis, Jr., California East of the Sierra, (Ph. D. thesis, University of California, unpub., 1942), p. 220.

[381]   California Assembly Journal, (1863-1864), p. 388.

[382]   Asa Merrill Fairfield, Fairfield's Pioneer History of Lassen County, California, (San Francisco, [1916]), p. 342.

[383]   Ibid., pp. 342-343.

[384]   Loc. cit.

[385]   California Assembly Journal, (1863-1864), pp. 430, 551, 677; California Senate Journal, (1863-1864), p. 489.

[386]   Statutes of California, 1863-1864, p. 264-269.

[387] Fairfield, op. cit., p. 313.

[388] Ibid., p. 259.

[389] Ibid., p. 297-298.

[390] Sacramento Union, December 27, 1861, p. 2.

[391] Fairfield, op. cit., p. 241.

[392] Ibid. p. 239.

[393] Ibid., p. 260.

[394] Edwin D. Hosselkus, [Ledger and Daybooks for a General Store in Susanville, California], MS 3 Vol., (Bancroft Library, University of California).

[395] Fairfield, op. cit., p. 358-361.

[396] Ibid., p. 367.

[397] Illustrated History of Plumas, Lassen and Sierra Counties, Fariss and Smith, pub., (San Francisco, 1882), p. 373. Hereinafter cited as Illustrated History.

[398] Fairfield, op. cit., p. 260.

[399] Illustrated History, op. cit., p. 386.

[400] Loc. cit.

[401] Loc. cit.

[402] Fairfield, op. cit., p. 409.

[403] Susanville Lassen Advocate, July 4, 1868, p. 3.

[404] Ibid., p. 2.

[405] Susanville Sagebrush as quoted in Fairfield, op. cit., p. 410.

[406] Fairfield, op. cit., p. 412.

[407] Carson City Territorial Enterprise, December, 1859, as quoted in Fairfield, op. cit., p. 207.

[408] Fairfield, op. cit., p. 283.

[409] Sacramento Union, November 18, 1861, p. 4. Roop made his point and the Council passed the bill with his recommendation included.

[410] Susanville Lassen Advocate, February 13, 1869, p. 3.

[411] Ibid., February 20, 1869, p. 2.

BIBLIOGRAPHY

I. Primary Sources

a. Manuscripts

Clemens, Orion, [Scrapbook, 1861-1864]. Microfilm in the Bancroft Library, University of California, Berkeley. A collection of clippings, notations and correspondence which Clemens assembled while a Nevada official.

Correspondence on the Boundary Question, 1863. California State Archives, Sacramento. A collection of official letters, telegrams and statements concerning the conflict between Roop County, Nevada and Plumas County, California in Susanville.

Executive Record [of Nevada Territory] 1861-1864. In U. S. Library of Congress, Records of the States of the United States (Nevada, microfilm, D. 2, Reel la, Unit 5). The film is in the University of Nevada Library, Reno. The document is a MS copy of the official business of the executive branch of the Territory of Nevada.

Fairfield, Asa Merrill, Fairfield Papers. California Section, State Library, Sacramento. A collection of letters and statements of pioneers of Lassen County collected by Fairfield when he was writing his history of the county.

Hosselkus, Edwin D. [Ledger and Daybooks for a General Store in Susanville, California]. 3 vols. Bancroft Library, University of California. Accounts for 1861-1864.

Jones, Israel, Dan Murray, Isaac Roop, Wm J. Young. "Report of a Joint Committee at Susanville." (February 16, 1863) in Correspondence on the Boundary Question, 1863. California State Archives, Sacramento.

"Memorial of the Citizens of Shasta, January 29, 1855," in Petitions to the Legislature, 1855. California State Archives, Sacramento.

Pierce, E. H., "Report of the Sheriff of Plumas County," (March 2, 1863), in Correspondence on the Boundary Question, 1863.

Roop House Register. California Section, State Library, Sacramento. A major source for life in the early days of Honey Lake. Entries form 1854 to 1860.

Roop, Isaac. [Book of Memoranda and Clippings]. A small book kept by Isaac Roop and now in the possession of his grandson, Mr. Medford R. Arnold of

Susanville. The major portion of Roop's collection of letters and papers disappeared after the turn of this century. Susan Roop Arnold consigned a box of papers to Asa Merrill Fairfield, but upon Mr. Fairfield's death shortly afterward, the box was gone.

Roop, Josiah. Josiah Roop's Business Records at Shasta, California. California Historical Society Library, San Francisco. Accounts for 1851-1852.

Territory of Nevada. Legislative Assembly. 1862. An Act [changing the name of Lake County to Roop County]. In the possession of Mr. Medford R. Arnold of Susanville.

Weatherlow, William. "Statement of William Weatherlow," in Fairfield Papers, California Section, State Library. A copy of Weatherlow's detailed statements concerning the Indian difficulties and relations in Honey Lake Valley, written before his death in 1864.

b. Government Documents

California.
Assembly Journal. 1855, 1856, 1862, 1863, 1864.
Senate Journal. 1853, 1855, 1862, 1863, 1864.
Statutes. 1850, 1852, 1858, 1859, 1860, 1861, 1863, 1864.

Nevada Territory.
Journal of the Council of the First Legislative Assembly of the Territory of Nevada, 1861.
Laws. 1861, 1862, 1863.

United States.
House Journal. 1858.
Statutes at Large. 1851, 1861, 1863, 1864.

Utah Territory.
Statutes. 1855.

c. Newspapers

Alta California. (San Francisco). 1851, 1852, 1857, 1859, 1862.

Daily Evening Bulletin. (San Francisco). 1857, 1858, 1861, 1863.

Lassen Advocate. (Susanville). 1868, 1869.

Sacramento Daily Union. 1852, 1857, 1859, 1861, 1862.

Shasta Courier. (Shasta). 1852, 1853, 1857.

Shasta Republican. (Shasta). 1858.

II. Secondary Sources

a. Articles

Bagley, Harry P. "Trouble on the Nevada Border," Sacramento Bee, November 4, 1939, magazine section, p. 3.

Blackmar, Charles M. "Notes on the Journal of P. B. Reading," Quarterly of the Society of California Pioneers, IX, (1932).

"A Brief Biography of Reading," Quarterly of the Society of California Pioneers, VII, (1930).

Bruce, A. T. "Isaac N. Roop," in Representative and Leading Men of the Pacific, Oscar T. Shuck, ed., (San Francisco, 1870), pp. 405-410.

Davis, William N., Jr. "The Territory of Nataqua, an Episode in Pioneer Government East of the Sierra," California Historical Society Quarterly, XXI, no. 3, (September, 1942), pp. 225-238.

Hershinsher, Beulah. "The Adjustment of the Boundaries of Nevada," First Biennial Report of the Nevada Historical Society, 1907-1908, (Carson City, 1909).

"A Jaunt to Honey Lake Valley and Noble's Pass," Hutchings' Illustrated California Magazine, Vol. I, June 1857, n. s. pp. 537-539. Based upon an account by John A. Dreibelbis, who accompanied Nobles.

Reading, Pierson B. "Journal of Pierson Barton Reading in His Journey of One Hundred Twenty-Three Days across the Rocky Mountains from Westport on the Missouri River, 450 Miles above St. Louis, to Monterey, California, on the Pacific Ocean, in 1843," Phillip Beakert, ed., Quarterly of the Society of California Pioneers, VII (1930), pp. 148-198.

Roop, Isaac. "Honey Lake Valley Correspondence," Shasta Republican, (1858). A series of letters to the paper telling of conditions in Honey Lake Valley.

Roop, Wendell. Isaac Roop Goes West. (n. p., 1958). A reprint furnished this writer by Mr. Roop of Sewall, New Jersey.

Shurtleff, Charles A. "Shasta," Quarterly of the Society of California Pioneers, VII, (1930), pp. 101-126.

Swartzlow, Ruby Johnson. "Peter Lassen, Northern California's Trail-Blazer," California Historical Society Reprints, (San Francisco, 1940).

Wells, Harry L. "The Sagebrush Rebellion," Overland Monthly, n. s. XIII, (March, 1889), pp. 197-212.

b. Books

[Angel, Myron, ed.] History of Nevada, Thompson and West, pub. (Oakland, 1881).

Bancroft, Hubert Howe. The Works of Hubert Howe Bancroft. XXI, (History of California, IV; San Francisco, 1882); XXIII (History of California, VI; San Francisco, 1888); XXV, (History of Nevada, Colorado, and Wyoming; San Francisco, 1890).

Beckwith, E. G. "Report of Explorations for a Route for the Pacific Railroad, of the Line of the Forty-first Parallel of North Latitude by Lieut. E. G. Beckwith, Third Artillery, 1854," Reports of Explorations and Surveys from the Mississippi River to the Pacific Ocean Made under the Direction of the Secretary of War in 1854-55. 33d Cong., 2d Sess., Sen. Exec. Doc., no. 78, Vol. II (Washington, 1855).

Browne, J. Ross. Report of the Debates in the Convention of California on the Formation of the State Constitution in September and October, 1849. (Washington, D. C., 1850).

Clemens, Samuel L. Mark Twain's Autobiography. (New York, 1924), 2 vols.

Coy, Owen C. California County Boundaries, (Berkeley, 1923).

Davis, William N., Jr. California East of the Sierra, A Study in Economic Sectionalism. (Ph. D. thesis, University of California, unpub, 1942).

Fairfield, Asa Merrill. Fairfield's Pioneer History of Lassen County, California. (San Francisco, 1916).

Frickstad, Walter N. A Century of California Post Offices, 1848 to 1954. (Oakland, 1955).

Giles, Rosena A. Shasta County, California, A History. (Oakland, 1949).

Guinn, J. M. History of the State of California and Biographical Records of the Sierras. (Chicago, 1906).

Hinkle, George and Bliss. Sierra-Nevada Lakes. (New York, 1949). American Lake Series, Milo Quaife, ed.

Illustrated History of Plumas, Lassen and Sierra Counties. Fariss and Smith, pub., (San Francisco, 1882).

Kroeber, A. L. Handbook of the Indians of California. Smithsonian Institution, Bureau of American Ethnology, Bulletin no. 78, (Washington, 1925).

Mack, Effie Mona. Mark Twain in Nevada. (New York, 1947).

Mack, Effie Mona. Nevada: A History of the State from the Earliest Times through the Civil War. (Glendale, California, 1936).

McNamar, Myrtle. Way Back When. (Cottonwood, California, 1954).

Read, Georgia Willis and Ruth Gaines, ed. Gold Rush. The Journals, Drawings and other Papers of J. Goldsborough Bruff, (Columbia University Press, 1944), 2 vols.

Russell, Israel C. Geological History of Lake Lahontan. A Quaternary Lake of Northwestern Nevada. U. S. Geological Survey Monographs, Vol. XI, (Washington, 1885).

Shinn, Charles H. Mining Camps. A Study in American Frontier Government. (New York, 1885).

Shuck, Oscar T. Representative and Leading Men of the Pacific. (San Francisco, 1870).

Twain, Mark. (Samuel Clemens). Roughing It. (Hartford, 1877 ed.).

Whitsell, Leon O. One Hundred Years of Masonry in California. (San Francisco, 1950).